All is in divine order!

Barbara Victoria

2005

Resolutions

A Story of Transformation
Through the Process of Loss

Cover Design: PRODESIGN
Published by Higher Shelf Publishing
an imprint of Pronghorn Press

HIGHER
SHELF
PUBLISHING

at
www.pronghornpress.org

Resolutions

To Naomi Yvonne Loman,
my first Hospice patient,
her husband, Johnny,
children Cathy, Little John,
Dana and Cheryl
and their families
and to Spirit Mountain Hospice,
Cody, Wyoming.

It is the 11th day of January 1991. My mother-in-law of twenty-three years has just been diagnosed with terminal cancer.

I first met Mary Fontaine Scott Foote on Easter Sunday of 1967, and we have been friends since. Her youngest son and I were married the following October and moved back to the family farm in central Kentucky seven years later— after graduate school, after Vietnam, after finishing graduate school, after three years in Pennsylvania where a daughter and son were born to us. We farmed with Mary and my father-in-law, Gerard Moore Foote, for three years, then bought them out with Jim's brother, Phillip. As part of the transaction, we deeded them twenty

Barbara Victoria

acres of adjoining land, land originally owned by Footes seven generations before us. It had been called Saratoga, and became Saratoga once again with a refurbished barn and the new home that Mary had always wanted. The folks moved into their new house in the fall of 1977 and we moved into the 100+ year-old farmhouse at Basin Spring, our children the fourth generation of the Foote family to live therein. Mary and Gerard looked after our pre-school son, Gerard, and first-grade daughter, Tessa, when I returned to work in the fall of 1978; we neighbored across the fields. By 1991 the children were in high school and college, almost grown. We had seen a lot together, now this.

This was the beginning of a watershed year. Mary's passage was the first of three odysseys of life and death that I would experience within twelve months. Informing each passage— to include both of my parents— was the substance of three singular lives.

Resolutions

Barbara Victoria

Resolutions

Mary

Barbara Victoria

Resolutions

1917—1991

Barbara Victoria

Resolutions

Bouquet

At 1:15 I awaken,
her son breathing softly beside me.
He handles it well by day
but at night his body constricts
ever so often as if he is battling
  the cancer that overtakes her
  daily

and I am awake wondering
what kind of night is she having
and did her headache subside and
is she awake wondering
  where is the headache coming from
  and will her daughter arrive
in time? Does she know —

I have always admired
  the way she sets a table
  the plants that flourish
    inside and outside her home

Barbara Victoria

her sheer delight in little ones
the utter sense of family
    that is her mantle

that I would bring my babies here again
    to grow up on this farm! Tomorrow
I will look for something at the florist's
a rose for her room
the dark eyes, the wide smile
the long tapering hands that have tended
hens and herbs and thirteen grandchildren

a rose for Mary's days.

Resolutions

Barbara Victoria

Resolutions

She was no stranger to cancer. A lump in her left breast had led to a radical mastectomy in the summer of 1965, leaving a scar that cut far deeper than breast tissue and lymph nodes. But this was different. On the 11th day of January in 1991 Mary had been given two weeks to two months to live. Period.

She met the news with grace and resolve. When I walked into the hospital room I found her propped up on pillows, resplendent in a cranberry velveteen robe brought to her by one of her grandsons, her silver hair swept away from the beautiful widow's peak and dark brown eyes. We did not say a word about the test, but it was all I could do to keep from crying as I leaned over the

Barbara Victoria

bed and hugged her. She smiled. We had come a long way together. And it was a long way from Stith Valley in Meade County where she was born and raised to the third floor of Baptist East Hospital in Louisville and this.

She was a country girl if there ever was one—married at sixteen, a mother at seventeen, and a mother of three before she turned twenty-one. Two more children would follow by the time her eldest daughter was fifteen.

Her young husband had come courting on horseback, a ten-mile ride from Basin Spring Farm to Scott Hill Farm nestled in Stith Valley where she grew up with two sisters and four brothers. They married on the last day of September shortly after her 16th birthday. By then the Great Depression held the country in a death grip, but not for two young newlyweds making their way in a horse-drawn wagon from Stith Valley to Basin Spring. A milk cow tethered to the wagon followed along behind.

The contents of that wagonload are long forgotten, save the tall oak wardrobe with beveled mirrors that now sits in the home of one

Resolutions

of her grandsons. But the old man—her husband of then fifty-four years—remembers a gay young girl riding by his side with the brown-eyed-Susan eyes, a cloud of honey blonde hair, and a smile that could defy fate. All of life lay before them under October skies.

Welcoming two babies in the midst of the Depression prompted a move to Detroit for him to find better opportunities for work. He was always able to find work. Far away from family and farm, they shared a house with another young couple also trying to make their way in a desperate time. A third baby arrived. They returned to Kentucky after Mary's father, the county sheriff, died of pneumonia after rescuing neighbors in the '37 flood. Her husband would farm. He would work. He would work and he would farm. And she would tend her plants and herbs and chickens and children, and later the grandchildren that would begin to arrive in her mid-thirties.

Cancer would strike again. She was a grandmother thirteen times and the great-grandmother of fourteen when an internist found

Barbara Victoria

the spot on her lung in September of 1990. Mary might have known better. Smoking grapevine back on the creek had been innocent enough at age fourteen, but she had been a cigarette smoker for most of her adult life. She moderated to a "lite" brand in later years and quit several years before the spot appeared, but the damage had already been done. The initial spot was found on her left lung in early September.

It had been a flawless late-summer day when Mary and I drove to Louisville to the doctor's office for a follow-up appointment. I do not remember now why it was she and I who went with no one else — maybe it had to do with farm work—but we treated it like a "girl trip." We had packed her overnight bag in case she was admitted, not wanting to repeat the fifty plus mile drive, and stopped for lunch at the King Fish, one of her favorite places to eat. Her mood was light, even after the doctor chose to admit her immediately to Baptist East Hospital. We were ready. She looked rather small in the hospital bed, but she was relaxed and looking forward to seeing her sons who lived in the

Louisville area.

We both felt good about what we had accomplished together that afternoon. It was not easy to leave her there, but we had faced the inevitable, done what we had to do, and were prepared to move forward. It had been a good day.

"I'll be back tomorrow," I said as I turned toward the door. "Is there anything else you need?"

"No, Barbara Allen. I'm fine. I'll rest here a little before Ed and Phil come by."

She had called me "Barbara Allen" for years after a character in the play, *Dark of the Moon*, that her daughter, Laura, and I had seen at the University of Kentucky's Guignol Theater when Jim was in Vietnam.

Surgery the next day took hours, it seemed, and there were several family members in the waiting room. I remember my father-in-law and my husband—the youngest son—sitting beside me, one of her brothers, and her sister, Jessie. Finally the doctor emerged from the operating room with good news and bad news. He had removed a tumor from the left lung and had taken it all. The bad news: a second tumor on the

Barbara Victoria

right lung was left alone—he did not think she could withstand both surgeries at the same time, opting for radiation to do the rest of the work. But she had come through the surgery well and the chest cavity surrounding the lungs was clear.

She recovered well at home, and thirty-three radiation treatments followed throughout the fall. Several family members helped with driving to the cancer center in Louisville, but most often it was my father-in-law who drove the 100 mile round trip, five days a week, two weeks at a stretch with a week off between cycles. It was a tiring regimen and she was depleted, but the treatments were finished just before Christmas.

A peaceful season it was. We decided to forego the annual family open house that we held in the old house where she had lived for nearly thirty years, where my husband and I and were entering our second decade. Upwards of sixty family members and neighbors would gather there between Christmas and New Year's, some contributing a covered dish and others bringing themselves. Invariably the groaning table featured Mary's sugar-glazed country ham, rum cake with pecan topping and glaze, and Kentucky jam cake with brown sugar icing. That season, however, we kept it simple. Mary snuggled into a Christmas sweatshirt that I had found for her emblazoned with "I Love You Deerly" and two reindeer on the front and spent the holiday reading and resting. She was tired. We were all tired, but we were glad to be together.

New Year's Day came and went. By the second week in January she was back in the hospital after she began feeling extremely tired and the internist thought she needed monitoring. This time she did not make it to Louisville, but was admitted by her internist in nearby Elizabethtown to the hospital there. The news was grave: cancer had spread into her skeletal system. She was given two weeks to two months to live.

How could this have happened so quickly? Except for the spot in her right lung, her chest cavity had been clear at the end of October! We were stunned.

The trips to Louisville for radiation

treatments resumed to control the pain, and to keep her mobile and her body functioning for as long as possible. Mary was adamant about remaining at home while the disease ran its course and we were determined to honor that. Hospice would be called in at the appropriate time.

Family members began dropping by regularly to visit. Her sister, Jessie, would arrive with a favorite dish or a book, and they would visit the way they had always done. Her granddaughter, Elizabeth, would spend an afternoon doing her nails. Her oldest daughter, Sue, would come up from Henderson for a few days to fix special dishes, putter with her about the house, and to take her to Louisville for treatments that week. Her youngest daughter, Laura, took her own daughter, Sarah, out of school and drove in from Casper, Wyoming, for a week—a risky prospect in the dead of winter. Her brothers would stop by, and her sons and grandsons with their families. Pictures were taken but no "good-byes" were uttered. It was about being present.

Resolutions

Be there...be there...be there.

In mid-February I had a run-in with viral pneumonia and spent four days in the hospital. Mary was beside herself.

"Barbara Allen! You've got to take care of yourself! You need to rest. Are you getting enough rest?"

I spent as much time with her as I could when I returned home from the hospital. Many afternoons I would walk across the fields to her house and find her propped up in her Jenny Lind bed in her bedroom that overlooked the bottomland along Sinking Creek. Books and magazines lay all about. She loved a good book and so did I, so I would ease into the recliner alongside her bed and we would read for a while until we both fell asleep. It never took long—I was so tired. She was so-o-o-o tired! And many evenings I would go back after supper to say goodnight before she dropped off to sleep.

Be there...be there... We were both healing our bodies and our spirits, but I was ever aware that we were treading different paths. I would recover in time; Mary had a different destination.

Barbara Victoria

Her energy waned as the weeks passed, and in late February the radiation treatments ceased. No more could be done. Jim called Laura in Wyoming.

"This is a good time to come back," he said.

"I was planning on coming in the second week in March during spring break," she replied. "If someone can meet me I'll fly into Louisville."

"Of course we can meet you!" he said, "Come on!"

It was a Friday the eighth of March when I stopped at Saratoga to see Mary on my way in from work and found the house bustling with activity. Sue had driven in from Henderson with her daughter-in-law, Marsha, a registered nurse. A nurse from Hospice was sitting on the sofa in the living room filling out papers to put Mary into the program. Mary was restless and uncomfortable, and her husband not at all in sync with the situation. In fact, he was more than a little annoyed by all the activity. *Who are all these people? And what is going on in my home?* Plenty was going on.

"The cancer has metastasized to the

Resolutions

brain," the Hospice nurse explained. "It's a matter of time now."

"How long?" we asked.

"It could be a few days, it could be several days," came the reply.

Laura and Jim arrived a little after nine that evening, and Laura went directly to her mother's bedside. By then Mary was beginning to slip in and out of consciousness. She had held on long enough to see her youngest daughter, and now we were all being swept forward on an immense tide.

Marsha was administering to Mary while Laura sat on the bed holding her mother's hands. Sue was sitting on the other side of the bed and I stood at the foot. Suddenly I felt like a bride again, planted in the midst of a very intimate scene within this family I had married into, daughters in the foreground, me on the periphery wondering what was appropriate.

Should I go, should I stay? What was the right thing to do?

I had embraced this family unequivocally —it was about heart, not genes. But there is a unspoken assumption in that region of the country that "blood is thicker than water." I had never been able to fully circumvent this no matter how much "heart" I put into it and this occasion was no exception. I looked at Marsha, who had married Mary's oldest grandson—they had been high school sweethearts. I had known Mary for twenty-five years; we had "neighbored" across the fields since my children were babies, and had shared in every phase of building the new house, its progress day by day with Mary's mounting enthusiasm. I had helped her move out of the old house and into the new one and hung pictures for her when the backbreaking work was done. It seemed I had as much reason to be there as anyone, but...

What to do? I did what I have always done at family functions through the years: I picked up the next task that beckoned—answer the phone, open the door, wash a dish, put on a pot of coffee...

Marsha led us into the basics of patient care, and the Hospice nurses—who had arrived none too soon that Friday afternoon—schooled us in what was taking place. Mary was actively dying. Our principal role was to keep her comfortable. Other than that, there was nothing we could do wrong, which seemed straightforward enough.

The first night was chaotic as we struggled to find a comfort zone for Mary and for ourselves. We each took turns "on watch," and were able to talk with her about how she was feeling and what she needed. Our work was cut out for us and it was not going to be easy. Sue and Laura took the brunt of the care-giving that night.

By the next morning we had settled into a routine that continued for five days and five nights as Mary completed the work of dying. Marsha was our advisor and our guide, our high priestess of patient care. We watched her interact with Mary and followed every move she made. Hospice checked in on us morning and afternoon and remained on call any time of the day or night for counsel or emergency.

By Saturday afternoon word had begun to spread through the community about what was taking place at Saratoga, and neighbors and friends began bringing food to the house. Mary's husband, Gerard, was slipping deeper into quandary about what was happening around him. *Who were all these people? What was going on in his home?*

The only son of an only son, Gerard Moore Foote was raised with four sisters who adored their only brother. He had been ninety-percent deaf for most of his adult life, so he had been more than culturally disposed as a Southern male to being waited upon by women. Suddenly his world had been upended. An army of women had commandeered his home and were revolving around his helpmate of more than five decades. Cars were coming and going out of his driveway, and people were in and out of his house. Life as he had known it had careened out of control.

What was happening to them? And what did it all mean?

We explained as gently as we could that the cancer had metastasized to Mary's brain and the disease would run its course. It could take

Resolutions

hours or it could take days. This did not sit well. He thought she should be in a hospital where doctors and nurses could care for her and keep her comfortable.

"Mama wants to stay at home and we are doing everything to see that she can," Sue explained. "We have Marsha and Hospice, and the hospital is only twenty minutes away if we need to take her there. We can handle everything here, Dad."

The old man wasn't buying it but he went along. There wasn't much else he could do.

Family members began arriving on and off on Sunday as more food arrived: casseroles, pies, cakes, a tray of cold cuts and cheese with fresh bread, a two-pound can of coffee which we began brewing around the clock. That evening I called my supervisor at work and explained what was taking place.

"The cancer has metastasized," I told her. "It will probably be a matter of days, but this is where I will be for as long as it takes," I explained, giving her the phone number at Saratoga.

"Do whatever you need to do," my

supervisor said, "and stay in touch. Let us know how it's going." I assured her that I would.

After hanging up the phone I raced down to the old farmhouse to pick up a few clothes and then hurried back to my in-laws. We had entered a new realm and I didn't want to miss anything that was taking place.

By Monday afternoon Mary was beginning to slip in and out of a dream state and was seeing things—cats on top of a cupboard, a favorite horse, loved ones of years ago.

"Go out of here, Shoo! Shoo!" she cried out, motioning the cats away with her hands. "Out! Out! Get out!"

I had heard of people "talking out of their heads" and that was what we were witnessing. Slices of Mary's life were playing out before her eyes. It was touching and amusing and it was wrenching. I wanted to go back in time with her, to stand by her side and see what she was seeing but it was not possible. Mary's life cinema was in replay.

I thought that I would remember always every detail of those five days and six nights, as

Resolutions

the woman who had been my friend, my comrade, my mentor on the farm and my mother-in-law, gradually withdrew from our world. Perhaps the details are not significant in themselves. What matters is the essence that the heart holds from those final days and nights.

Marsha had to return to Henderson after a couple of days, leaving Sue and Laura and I as "nurses." We were on our own. That was a breathtaking prospect, but Hospice remained a lifeline for us as we did what we could to keep Mary comfortable. Sue and Laura attended to her physical needs and encouraged her to eat. Sometimes a spoonful was all she could manage. After a few days all she would take was a sip of liquid or the few ice chips we could give her to keep her mouth from drying out.

On the third day since the cancer metastasized the Hospice nurse advised us to have a hospital bed moved into the room. It would make Mary more comfortable and make it easier for us to take care of her. Hospice covered the cost; all we had to do was make a call to have it delivered. We were floored. What an amazing organization, this Hospice! I was wholly in awe.

The arrival of the bed caused a flurry of activity. Whatever skills I lacked as a nurse I certainly could make up for moving furniture and wielding a screwdriver, and Laura and I went into high gear. We eased Mary into the hospital bed and wheeled it to one side of the room. The Jenny Lind had to go, and we began taking it apart and hauled it into the adjoining bedroom where we reassembled it again.

The hospital bed looked small and clinical compared to Mary's antique, but once it was in place where she could look out at the fields we were thoroughly pleased. Moreover, we could raise and lower the head, and adjust the height with the push of a button to easily turn or bathe her. What relief! For a crowning touch I searched through the closet for a pretty spread and came upon Aunt Jessie's appliqued "Tree of Life" quilt that we spread across the bed, and drew up to Mary's chest. It was as perfect as we could make it.

The adjoining bedroom was arranged dormitory style. The two antique double beds were moved side by side, and we put the day bed

Resolutions

by the window. Now everyone had a place to sleep in the same room, and Mary was close in the adjoining bedroom. It was a buoyant moment. We had embraced the task before us, and were now equipped to be, if not nurses, the best caregivers we could be.

Friends and neighbors continued to respond bringing food and flowers and encouragement. My father-in-law was still baffled by the attention and annoyed by the constant interruptions, but I believe he began to see that our lives were changing forever and people were rising to the occasion. He started to relax, and he began relieving us on our "watches." Seating himself beside her bed he would take Mary's slender hand into his own great palm.

"This is Gerard. I'm taking care of you now," he would say in the gravelly voice that was unmistakably his. This was the extent of his "taking care" during those days and nights, but it was a relief to have him there, and, moreover, to know that he was coming to terms with the realm we all had entered.

The next afternoon I made an excursion to the outside world to procure a potty-chair. Mary could no longer get to the bathroom nor could she talk to us, and she would become frantic at the prospect of soiling herself or her bed linens. The chair helped during the day when two of us could ease her into and out of it, but nighttime was a different story. Sue and Laura were exhausted.

"Y'all get some sleep," I told them. "I'll take over. If I run into anything I'll let you know."

That seemed simple enough. I lay down in the recliner by the bed in Mary's room until I began to hear her stirring about. I knew what this meant and I was ready. As frail as she had become, it should not be a problem easing her into and out of the chair. I was utterly wrong.

Lifting Mary from the bed down onto the chair was more than awkward. She could not help at all, though she knew what was happening as I struggled to support her entire weight with all the muscle I could muster. I was trying not to drop her.

"Come on, darlin'," I cajoled as I

positioned my feet and clasped my hands around her back. She looked at me with those brown eyes and I could read her thoughts. *Barbara Allen! Can't you do this any better than this?*

"Believe it or not, I'm doing the best I can. We can do this now."

When the mission was accomplished I thought the crisis was over but I was wrong about that, too. Getting Mary back into bed was no easier than getting her out. Determined not to disturb Sue and Laura, I eased and hauled and pulled and tugged until somehow I managed to ease Mary back onto the bed. She lay back exhausted. The bed was a wreck, I had not been able to wipe her, and her gown was every which-way.

"We'll deal with the rest of this later. I will make it up to you, I promise," I said to her.

I straightened her gown, the sheets and blankets, disturbing her as little as possible, and pulled the covers up around her.

Wherever she is now, I hope that Mary has forgiven me that night. Moreover, I hope that Barbara Allen's nursing prowess gave her a good laugh.

Day four. We had begun to see changes in Mary's responsiveness and overall condition. She was refusing food, she was incommunicative, and she was sleeping more and more. We asked Hospice what it meant and were given the second most important lesson that I learned from Hospice: hearing is the last faculty to go.

"Don't talk around the patient as if he or she cannot hear you," the nurse cautioned. "This is not the case. It is a good time to say things you want to impart while you can. Keep your loved one comfortable and give them your love. Take care of yourselves as well."

As the nurse explained the guideposts to look for as life waned, I was thunderstruck by the parallels to the Lamaze course I had taken nearly two decades before to bring two babies into the world. After Lamaze I knew a good deal about the birthing process; it had been the most comprehensive learning experience of my entire life. Death was all new to me.

I wasn't particularly afraid of death—I just didn't have a handle on it at all. I had attended

Resolutions

my first funeral as a bride of three weeks when my husband's grandfather passed away. I had no idea how to react as we walked into the funeral home where the body of the elderly gentleman I had met only a few times lay carefully presented in a casket. A mass of new relatives rushed forward to greet us, and I was paralyzed not knowing what to say or what to do, stationed between the deceased and the living. Bizarre, indeed, this business of death. In practical terms I had it all to learn.

We were agile students at Mary's bedside, though taking care of ourselves became an increasing challenge. Between family and neighbors we received a lot of support, but it was real physical and emotional work. There were indelible moments, however, and late night "girl talk" in our dormitory room while another was on watch. The sheer intensity of what we were engaged in together brought forth feelings and experiences that had not been aired at any other time. It was, in the words of Charles Dickens, "the best of times and the worst of times."

By day four we were having problems.

Mary was fitful, and we had done all we could do for her. Something definitely was not right, and finally we called Hospice. The nurse arrived to examine her and discovered that her bowels were impacted. Not only had she been enduring that discomfort for days, the morphine pills that Sue and Laura had been giving her rectally were impacted as well. Her blood stream had absorbed nothing; she had been in pain for days with no way to tell us.

We were aghast. In the one thing we had been tasked to do—to keep her comfortable—we had failed.

The nurse performed an enema and gave Mary an injection of morphine. Sue and Laura cleaned her up, slipped on a fresh gown, and tucked her in again. The nurse said Hospice would deliver liquid morphine to the house. This would ease her pain. But it would hasten the end for her as well.

Mary rested well all that afternoon. She was showing signs, however, that her system was beginning to shut down. What little urine we collected was dark in color, and the nurse said

Resolutions

that death would not be long. We called her sons in Louisville, her brothers, her beloved sister, Jessie, and other relatives and friends who would want to know.

That evening remains one of the most memorable of my life. Mary had assumed what Hospice termed "the death mask" as she lay on her back. Her mouth was partially open, and occasionally you could hear a sound in her throat, the "death rattle" we were told. She was dressed in her favorite gown, with the "Tree of Life" quilt spread from her chin to her feet. We had done all that we could do.

Family members began arriving late in the afternoon and stayed well into the evening. The lamps were turned low and made the room glow as one after another came back and sat with her. Others gathered around the table in the dining room and in the living room. The lamplight was cozy and there was a murmur of conversation. Everyone knew the immediacy of the moment, but there was a sense of buoyancy as well. We were all where we needed to be and the collective energies resonated like any gathering for

Barbara Victoria

Thanksgiving or Easter Sunday. She had brought us together as a family, as always, at home over food and conversation. All was in divine order.

Mary's scene, Mary's night. We basked in the gift that was her last. I cannot remember all the faces that night—I know that her brothers Jimmy and Jack were there, her sister Jessie, her granddaughter Elizabeth, and friends and neighbors. A few people stayed away, preferring to remember Mary as she had been; vibrant and alive. I found this curious and a little offensive, but it held another of the great lessons of that time: every contribution matters. Every gesture, every thought people are able to call forth reverberates on both sides of the earth plane during a transition. That is all that matters.

A few stayed the night. Aunt Jessie stationed herself in the recliner by Mary's bed. Sue and Laura and I prepared to get some rest (though no one did for long). Jim slept on the couch in the living room, his father in the basement room he had inhabited since Mary became sick and the extra bedroom upstairs became occupied by visiting family. Our son,

Resolutions

Gerard—named for his grandfather—came into her bedroom carrying his sleeping bag.

"We're goin' campin,' Grandmama," he said, unrolling the sleeping bag on the floor at the foot of her bed. There was not a dry eye in the room. We each knew that this would be her last night with us. Her symptoms were final. She had stopped eating entirely the day before and her kidneys were shutting down. She was comatose. The Hospice nurse said that death could occur at any time.

The next morning everyone who needed to leave left for the day. Jim went to work at the bank, Gerard to high school. There was no change for Mary, breathing laboriously through her open mouth. We made her as comfortable as we could and settled into the morning.

Aunt Jessie left for her home in Elizabethtown around quarter after three. Mary's condition seemed stable, and Aunt Jessie said she had a few things to do.

"I'll be back this evening," she said.

It was down to Sue and Laura and Mary and me. Gerard, Sr. and Sue's husband, CH, were in the dining room talking. Mary's breathing was labored but steady. Her face was pale. She was no longer the Mary we knew but her body was still with us.

The past five days had taken their toll. We were all tired. There wasn't anything more we could do. We had to keep-on-keeping-on, but for how long? How long could Mary hold up? Dying is hard work, real labor, and she had been laboring for days.

Laura was sitting on the end of the bed and Sue near the head of the bed holding Mary's hand. I was perched on a low stool on the other side of the bed and held her right hand in mine, my thumb on the pink abalone ring that my husband and I had given her following a trip to New Mexico a few years before.

"I wish she didn't have to suffer any more," Sue said. "It's so hard on her!" She started to cry. We all began to cry. Suddenly the words of the Hospice nurse flashed through my mind.

Hearing is the last faculty to go... I leaned over and put my lips near her right ear and whispered, "Yes, Yes!!" It was right for her to go.

# Resolutions

It was right for us to let her go. It was time.

That stands out as one of the most significant acts of my entire life. I wanted her to hear me. I wanted her to hear all of us. I wanted her to know that if she needed to let go it was all right, that we all wished her peace. What I did not realize as I sat there with her daughters, her hand in mine, was that we had just given her permission to let go. Moreover, she needed that permission as much as we needed to be released, but we all had to arrive there together. This was the point that we had all been working toward those final days and nights. Our final gift to her and her to us. It was now time for each of us to move forward.

Within minutes Mary's breathing slowed. Her mouth began to close slightly. I looked at Sue, and Sue looked at Laura. This was it.

Sue called out to her father and husband in the other room, "Dad, CH, come quick! Something's happening!" They rushed into the bedroom, and the five of us were transfixed as Mary's breathing gradually reduced to a whisper.

At ten minutes after four on the

Barbara Victoria

thirteenth day of March 1991, Mary Fontaine Scott Foote drew her last breath.

The vigil was over.

I slipped out of the bedroom and began doing the only thing I knew to do: I called Jim at the bank, Edwin and Phillip in Louisville, Aunt Jessie and Uncle Jimmy and Uncle Jack and Uncle Bill, Aunt Frannie and Uncle Charlie, granddaughters, grandsons... And to cousin Sonny Alexander at the funeral home in Irvington.

A slow drizzle set in during the afternoon as family and friends began arriving again. Coffee was brewed. Food was laid out. One by one they came back to sit at her bedside to bear witness to the woman who had been mother, grandmother, sister, cousin and friend. Unlike the night before, that had been nearly convivial, voices were subdued and tender.

Sonny arrived as dusk was gathering. Slowly, Mary's body was eased onto a gurney and covered. Family members moved it down the hall and out the front door to the waiting hearse. Several of us gathered on the front porch. Jim

came around the right corner of the house and through the yard as a light rain fell. He was wearing his Stetson hat. His cheeks were tracked with tears.

I heard a whinny and turned to the left to see my father-in-law's Tennessee walking horse, a strapping strawberry roan, standing by the fence. Strawberry was telling us, "I am with you." Stuey, our black lab, worked his way up on to the porch, and I felt a warm pressure on my left leg as he leaned into me and sat down on my left foot. He, too, was saying, "I am here and I know what you are feeling." We stood together in silence watching the taillights of the hearse grow smaller as it climbed the drive in the falling rain. Mary was leaving home for the last time.

That night I awoke in the dark. The house was still, except for the breathing of Laura and Sue in the beds in our "dormitory" room, and the ticking of the antique clock coming from the living room. Mary was gone, but all was in divine order. I felt an unusual warmth in my chest that began spreading through me. It was peaceful and relaxing, and soon I fell back to sleep.

Barbara Victoria

The following morning I finally left the house and drove down the hill to our farm where I called my mother in Maine. I told her how we had been consumed the last five days and that Mary had just died. My mother's mother, Stella, had been dead two years when I learned of her passing. I knew why, but I was dumbstruck after what I had just been through; How could my mother have kept it to herself? Feeling the enormity of what she had borne, I broke into tears.

"How," I wailed, "could you bear the loss of your mother alone? Why didn't you tell me at the time?" I sobbed.

"Now, now, dear," she said with her soothing mother-voice, "pull yourself together." Then she gave me another singular piece of advice from that watershed time.

"Don't think about everything at once. Just take one thing at a time," she said. "We'll talk about it. We'll talk about all of it later." There would be no "later," but she had told me what I needed to hear.

Details crowded the rest of the day: What should Mary wear? Sue and Laura took care of that, and selected a pretty outfit and an expensive pair of shoes that she had never worn. Tessa and I took care of her "foundations." We all agreed that Mary should have something new and pretty "to go to Paradise." Sue thought red would be nice, her favorite color. "Wouldn't it be fun to get her a red teddy," she mused. So, after living on another planet for more than a week, I ventured into the world again with my daughter Tessa, who had come in from college, and we drove the thirty miles to shop for Mary at the mall in Elizabethtown.

I remember feeling drained and red-eyed from where we had been and what lay ahead as we made our way across the parking lot to the department store, but we got right down to business. A red teddy it was, with half-slip to match. Wow! We were feeling pretty proud of ourselves for finding exactly what we wanted right off the bat and carrying it off without breaking into either laughter or tears. Then we ran into at a particularly garrulous woman from Breckinridge County who rushed over to us.

"What are ya'll doin'?" she chirped.

Barbara Victoria

Tessa and I looked wanly at one another. I did not know if the woman knew that Mary had died and I certainly could not go into the specifics of our mission. *How to pull this off*, I wondered.

"Oh, uh, we're just looking around," I said lamely, trying not to be engaged in conversation any longer than necessary. We needed to get out of there before we ran into anyone else, and, mercifully, we did.

It was comforting to return to the familiar world we had been immersed in for the last week. I took Mary's pretties to the funeral home with clothes Sue and Laura had gathered and returned the next morning to do a final check before the wake and funeral that afternoon. I was dreading what I might see—her mouth had been contorted with labored breathing for the last two days. But the body that lay before me had been transformed under the skilled hands of the undertaker and a cousin who is a hairdresser.

Mary was dressed in a pretty blouse and skirt and was nicely made up, with her silver hair swept away from the beautiful widow's peak. Her tapering hands were gently folded at her lap. I felt

Resolutions

oddly detached, however, as I looked down at the face I had known for more than twenty-five years. It was Mary, but it was not Mary. Her spirit may have been with us at that time, but it had left the body that lay before me. The features I knew so well seemed to belong to someone else, and suddenly I knew that I could handle what lay before us that day. The others could, too.

She had the most beautiful hands — small palms with long tapering fingers. Her nail beds were long and made her nails look elegant whether or not they were trimmed. Usually she wore polish which made them even more elegant. I wanted to try to capture those hands forever in a drawing and took a pencil and paper to the funeral home when I went to check her makeup.

Hands are one of the most difficult parts of the human body to render on paper. and I sat by the casket drawing, and erasing, and beginning again. Finally I folded my drawing tablet. It was no use. I could not capture the grace of those hands any more than I could fully recognize the body that lay before me as Mary. It would have to be enough to remember them as I did her.

It was Sunday, St. Patrick's Day, a very March day of wind and rain. Sons and daughters and grandchildren and scores of neighbors and friends joined together for the funeral service in Irvington. The "Tree of Life" quilt was draped over an antique chair by the casket. Family members took part in the service conducted by her sister-in-law, the Reverend Alice Bondurant Scott. A long procession of cars wended through the rolling countryside from the funeral home in Irvington to the Cap Anderson Cemetery just outside of Brandenburg in her native Meade County. A brief graveside service was conducted as she was laid near the graves of her parents, Walter and Ruth Scott, and her sister Rena Lou Scott Parks. Afterwards her family and friends returned to the farm in Breckinridge County for dinner.

Pure Mary.

After the funeral, the rhythms of work and farm and raising children resumed. I sought out Sylvia Willett, a friend of mine, and a spiritual healer who told me two significant things. Most

Resolutions

startling, she said that Mary had visited each of us during the night after she died to make sure we were all right. My mind flashed back to the warm feeling I had experienced when I had awakened that very night. The heart chakra, the center of love in the body, had been resonating with her presence. Sylvia added that some time in the future Mary would send a sign that she was all right, and that I would know when this occurred.

Several months later, in early fall, I was walking on the farm just before dark. The sun had just slipped below the horizon and the Evening Star shone alone in the sky. Suddenly I felt Mary's presence surround me. This was the moment that Sylvia had foretold! Mary was home and she was fine. I grinned at the evening star.

My step was lighter as I walked back to the old house in the gathering dusk.

Barbara Victoria

Resolutions

September Soup

Give me a picture of him
to keep forever, forever
this white-haired man
dressed in work pants and a pajama top
bent over his soup bowl,
autumn filtering through the air
with the last rays of afternoon.

The flowers on the table
 gathered in the yard
were transplanted by her
from the house where they lived for 30 years.
 The fragrance is old-fashioned, like her
 The flowers are her
 this balmy evening.

They were married sixty years ago
 on the last day of September;
she was just sixteen, he twenty-one.

Barbara Victoria

I want to ask
did they plan it in the steamy evenings
   of July and August
or did they just run off to Brandenburg
to the Methodist church
on a warm evening in 1933,
a night laced with equinox
   a night like this one
nine months before the first of
five children arrived.

The flowers say
she is here
the light filtering in the back porch window says
she is here
his quietness says she is here
as he bends over his soup

vegetable soup she would have made
thickened with okra, tomatoes, corn,
rich with soup bone. He learned to make it
   after she died of cancer. Angry
   that she would go before him.

Resolutions

he also learned to wash his clothes,
clean the bathroom, and
sweep the kitchen floor. Eighty years old
   his last birthday
he still does all his yard work, grows his garden
   that could feed four families
tends horses, and cattle.
He still sleeps in the basement
where he retreated while she lay dying,
the upstairs bedrooms filled
   with daughters and grandchildren
   her sister
   there to see her
      to paint her nails, brush her hair
      to read to her
   or sit by the bed as she dozed
to the end of her life
their life

to rooms empty of her
save an old-fashioned fragrance
that wafts through the air
while he sleeps downstairs.

Barbara Victoria

Resolutions

Victoria

Barbara Victoria

Resolutions

1917—1991

Barbara Victoria

Resolutions

Visiting Victoria

My mother had the warmest hands
  this side of Paradise.
She is the only person I know
who would cover a brick with embroidered linen
  and tie it with a lavender velvet ribbon
    for a doorstop

my mother is the only person I know who would
mend a bath towel with a rainbow patch
  on both sides of the hole,
and paint the legs of a canvas stool
    with tiny flowers

my mother is the only person I know
who has seashells in every room,
a cupid playing the mandolin
  on her bathroom door
and fall leaves pressed between waxed paper
  pinned to her curtain year around

Barbara Victoria

my mother is the only person I know
with more than one sewing basket,
who would sew felt needle holders and heart-shaped
  pin cushions, and decorate them with
  embroidery and beads

my mother is the only person I know
who would keep a tablecloth for 40 years
  and still use it,
who would make her own envelopes and note paper
  and write all around the margins

my mother is the only person I know
who would have pictures of cats
  and pillows of cats
    and not have a cat,
and pictures of a child she babysat
  with her children and grandchildren
  in frames she decorated by hand

my mother is the only person I know
who would sew by hand
  potholders and pillows and
  curtains and nightgowns,

Resolutions

and doll clothes with French seams,
and dolls for her grandchildren.

My mother is the only person I know
who could bear her mother's death alone,
move from Kentucky to Maine
   in a little blue Volkswagen
      days before Christmas,
take her grandchildren to the park
   when she could not walk,
read when she could not sew,
sew when she could not cry,
dream of the ocean all her life,
laugh in her last photograph.

Barbara Victoria

Resolutions

*F*our and a half months later the call came from my oldest brother, Charles, on a shining summer morning shortly before noon. I had just returned from securing two weeks of leave from work, two weeks to back off, let down, and regroup from a reduction-in-force that was sweeping Fort Knox and the ensuing office politics that had become crushing. I was relieved until my brother's words rent the flawless summer morning.

"Mother is dead," he said.

I was utterly stunned. *How could such a force be stilled?*

"No, no!" I wailed into the phone. It could

Barbara Victoria

not be. "Not Mother. Not Victoria!"

"I'm at her apartment. I found her body on the floor. I'm waiting for someone to come help move it," he said.

It was the 30th of July, six days before our mother's seventy-fifth birthday.

She was the daughter of Polish immigrants. Her father, Stefan Ochenkoski (OH-HEN-kos-ki) immigrated as a youth from Ostrolenka, a small town near the Russian border. He had left behind two sisters, and put away money for years to bring them to America. In 1939 he wrote to them saying that he had enough for passage if they would come. His letter crossed the Atlantic as Germany invaded Poland. No word came from Ostrolenka. There would be no word from Ostrolenka again.

Years later Stefan learned of a Polish priest who had immigrated to Chicago from Ostrolenka and he traveled to Chicago to meet him. It was a huge undertaking for him at the time, financially and emotionally, but he wanted to learn what he could of his sisters.

"You do not want to know what

happened," the priest said darkly. "Everything is gone. There is nothing left."

Several years before I heard this story I visited the Holocaust Memorial in Washington, D.C. and had an arresting experience. The enormity of the exhibits, the hush throughout the museum were punctuated only by the shuffling of feet and occasional whispering. I was dumbstruck, however, by a wall-sized photograph depicting a scene from the early years of the Nazi occupation of Poland. It showed a wooded landscape backlit by rays of a predawn sky as the sun rose just below the horizon. Figures could be made out fleeing into the trees as daylight threatened to expose them to view.

I was looking at the Polish countryside. As I studied one terrifying moment in a horrific era, the hair rose on the back of my neck in a way that I could not explain. I understood why several years later when my brother told me the story of our grandfather and his sisters. I recalled that the Nazis had gone after the Poles first, Polish Catholics like the Ochenkoskis, and my mind flashed back to the shadowy figures in the

Barbara Victoria

woods. They may well have been my great-aunts, their friends and families who had been living quiet lives in a Polish border town historically vulnerable to attack. There was no way of knowing, however. There had been no sunrise for the Poles in the photograph just as there had been no word from Stefan's sisters after the outbreak of World War II. History had swallowed them all.

Stefan married another immigrant, Stella Dougolenski, and eight children were born to them in Port Washington, N.Y., where they lived in a Polish community on Long Island. Stefan worked as a gardener on the posh Long Island estates of wealthy landowners and entertainers, such as Hollywood comedian Eddie Cantor; Stella took in their laundry while raising six sons and two daughters.

Victoria was the eldest. Early on she held a vision of herself that was larger than the confines of her ethnic community. According to Polish custom, she was allowed to select a middle name when she reached the age of communion in the Catholic Church, and she chose for herself the name Barbara. When I asked her why, she said offhandedly that it was the name of a movie star at the time. That is how she and I became Victoria Barbara, and Barbara Victoria.

As the firstborn, Victoria shouldered responsibility for the care of her seven siblings. They held her in awe, and indeed the venerable sister had her hands full. Reading became a haven to escape the clamor of family, as were the salt-water beaches off Sands Point and Montauk Point where she loved to walk.

The economics facing a large immigrant family were formidable, and the Ochenkoskis were forced to move often. The neighborhood joke was, "There go the Ochenkoskis again." The term "Polak" was ugly to Victoria. You wouldn't say it around her or tell Polish jokes. Neither was amusing to her.

My mother was an excellent student in high school but at Stella's insistence she withdrew after the 11th grade to help support the family. This entailed commuting by train from Port Washington into "the city"—Manhattan— where she worked as a dental assistant in

Barbara Victoria

Rockefeller Center. One of her youngest brothers, my Uncle Henry, said that she would come home and line up all her young siblings and show them how to brush and floss their teeth.

Victoria took pride in her work, but she longed to finish high school, and planned to enroll for her senior year the following fall. Stella blocked her every step of the way, so Victoria Barbara kept her job in the city working for Dr. Brown until she married my father at age twenty-two. My father was not Catholic—in fact, he had never been baptized—and Stella was outraged. Victoria left the Catholic church and she and my father became Episcopalians. She never graduated from high school, but was widely read and erudite throughout her life. The rift with her mother, however, became bitter and lifelong.

The Ochenkoskis spoke fluent Polish at home, but Victoria was adamant about being American. She rarely looked back after she left Port Washington, and called herself an "unabashed flag waver." Her children were never drawn into her heritage, and my brothers and I

Resolutions

knew little of our Polish family, with the exception of Uncle Henry and Uncle John, who came into our lives at different times. I saw my grandmother, Stella, three times, perhaps, and met my grandfather Stefan once. He visited us in Delaware on Silverside Road when I was about six years old, and enthralled us with Polish polkas on his concertina. The rest of the family was lost to us, like the shadowy figures fleeing into the Polish woods, like my great-aunts whose names were lost as well.

Victoria O. Guilford reinvented herself as a wife, homemaker, and mother of three in suburban Delaware. My father's income as a court reporter afforded her a comfortable life, full with PTA and Girl Scouting and volunteer work and all the challenges of raising children. There would be a large two-story Cape Cod home with a two-car garage for a yellow and white station wagon and my father's spiffy MGA convertible, a sunny yellow cottage within walking distance of Delaware Bay for summers of swimming and sailing, and a Sailfish with a red and white striped sail that I raced on Sunday afternoons at the

Barbara Victoria

Lewes Yacht Club on Delaware Bay. After three summers I finally won a race, an invitational at Indian River Inlet, and brought home a silver platter with four tiny legs to my dumbfounded family, who on this rare occasion, had stayed home and missed the race.

The marriage lasted twenty-three years. Victoria was not prepared for it to end. She and my father had soldiered through the most prosperous years of their marriage into the separation that shattered Victoria for the rest of her life. The indomitable Polish will, however, would not be broken. It carried her forward through a time when there were no cultural terms for "displaced homemaker."

Victoria met circumstance with grit and class. Her work was, for the most part, relegated to caretaking positions—as a housemother for sororities and fraternities on college campuses, as a caregiver of the elderly and infirm in their richly appointed homes on manicured estates, as a sitter for the children of doctors and professors and other professionals. She chose her jobs well, and when necessary put her furniture in storage to move on to a better opportunity.

In December of 1986, she drove a little blue Volkswagen "beetle" from Kentucky to Maine where she settled for the remaining years of her life. She moved into a retirement complex, and furnished her apartment with treasures that had managed to survive the years of moving and storage. She lived close to the Morgan Bay and the ocean, where she could enjoy the bracing salt air and the ebb and flow of the Atlantic surf. It took only minutes to visit my brother and his family where she relished the company of her infant granddaughter and grandson, sharing with them wonders of walks along the beach, books and puzzles, and the innovative surprises that distinguished her grandmother-style. She was a central figure in their lives, and these were undoubtedly the happiest years of her life—since the days when she had been a young homemaker raising children of her own.

I had talked with her on Sunday morning, two days before Charles called with his awful announcement. Her right knee, which had been injured in a fall on the ice many years before, was

Barbara Victoria

badly swollen and feverish. Her family doctor assured her that it was not phlebitis—my initial concern—but she could barely get around and could not drive the little blue Volkswagen. The doctor had referred her to the East Maine Regional Medical Center for tests the following Tuesday afternoon.

"I am glad you are getting it checked," I told her, "and right away. You can't take a chance with something like this." We rambled on about other things, then came back to the appointment. "What time do you go in?" I asked. Her appointment was at 1 p.m. and my brother was to take her. "I'll call you after that."

There was an awkward hesitation, and I cannot remember what either one of us said afterwards—probably something like, "Take care of yourself," followed by, "Oh, I will," and "I'll call you Tuesday." But I vividly remember wishing I had told her I loved her. It is not something that was often said between us and a singular feeling washed over me. I was worried about phlebitis and was very concerned. *I'll tell her when I call on Tuesday*, I had thought to myself. Still, I had the feeling that something had been left undone.

These thoughts ran through my head as I bolted from the house into the sunshine after hanging up the phone from Charles' call and ran towards the barn where my sixteen-year-old son was cleaning out stalls.

"Gerard, Gerard!" I began calling to him from the top of the spring. I was crying when I reached him. "Grandmother Vicky has died!" He wrapped his arms around me and I put my head on his chest and sobbed.

I flew alone to Maine. Money was tight, but I wish I had insisted that my family go. Though my children had not spent time with Grandmother Vicky on a daily basis as they had with Mary, she was a distinct presence in their lives. Packing for the trip, I tucked in a couple of poems to read if the occasion arose—one for my family in Kentucky and one about the farm. It occurred to me that I might write another just for her, but I didn't want to to churn out something saccharin just for the occasion; however, something might present itself and I was open

Barbara Victoria

to that.

Interestingly, my mother had sent me a clipping a couple of months before regarding a national poetry contest that she thought might be of interest. That was unusual for her. She had never particularly acknowledged my writing— too much risk—why now? I had never written for a contest, let alone entered one, so I put the clipping aside. Weeks later I found it, however, and for some reason changed my mind. I just happened to have a poem that fell within the prescribed line length and it was also one of my favorites. I sent it off like a missile into outer space and never gave it another thought, nor did I mention it to anyone, not even to my mother.

My oldest brother met me at the airport in Bangor. Charles, eldest son, the prince of the family who seemed more like ten years older than I was rather than three. I had worshipped him while we were growing up. He majored in forestry at Duke for two years, then architecture for two more years at Carnegie Tech before heading West when the college money ran out to work in the oil fields of Big Piney, Wyoming.

Resolutions

After several years he returned to school in Laramie and earned two degrees in English at the University of Wyoming where he subsequently taught, then headed to San Francisco to study Zen at Tassajara Springs. After several years in California he moved to Maine to study with a Zen master at Surry and, after teaching English briefly on the college level, began working as a master carpenter doing finish work on multimillion-dollar yachts for the Hinkley Shipyard in Southwest Harbor. At age forty he married a fellow Zen student, and he and Susan began raising a family.

Charles and I putzed around town until our middle sibling, Richard, arrived on a later flight from Virginia. Richard Coeur de Lion we called him—Richard the Lion-Hearted. He and I were born fourteen months apart and were referred to as "The Kids" by our parents and Charles, who seemed to us to enjoy the status of a quasi-adult. Richard had been born prematurely, his nervous system underdeveloped, and I wonder if that had affected him permanently. He could be an excellent student, and had a soaring

Barbara Victoria

IQ, but his grades tended to reflect his interests, not the steady precision of a scholar. His sensitive soul found refuge in books and he read voraciously, everything from comic books to medieval history. He would lose himself in tales of knighthood and chivalry, and would labor for hours over intricate drawings in pen and ink showing knights in armor, knights on horseback, knights with plumed helmets and full battle paraphernalia. Sensitive to a fault, he was shattered by our parents' separation in the spring of his senior year in high school, and spent the following year—and most of his adult life—in and out of mental hospitals. The diagnosis, bi-polar disorder with schizophrenic features, was concluded well into his fourth decade.

The three of us drove to the funeral home in Brewer where our mother's body had been taken. I followed my brothers into the room where she lay, noticing their thinning pates. Her Terrible Trio, as she called us, had arrived looking very middle-aged.

Victoria had sewn all her life and had taken to hand sewing special items for herself,

Resolutions

and doll clothes with French seams for her granddaughters. We found our mother clad in a cotton gown she had sewn by hand. Her hair was clean and swept back from the Slavic brow and cheekbones that I knew so well. As with Mary a few months before, I beheld my mother, but it was not her. The larger-than-life persona of Victoria, the consummate Leo, had been stilled. Though overweight for most of her adult life, she appeared amazingly small. Perhaps death does that to us. Her overall frame looked diminutive, especially her feet.

I needed to see her to believe it, and it was true: Mother was dead.

My brothers and I talked about what to do next as we drove to Charles' and Susan's home near Surry, just south of Ellsworth. We had been raised in the Episcopal Church—a comfortable alliance for a defected Catholic—and Richard wanted an Episcopalian funeral. Charles was practicing Zen Buddhism and I was, for lack of a better term, a New Age spiritualist, so this would be challenging. A Terrible Trio we presented, indeed.

Barbara Victoria

After supper with Charles' family he took me to our mother's. I wanted to stay there, and was utterly exhausted when he dropped me off and drove home. But my entry into the world she had left behind is one of my most vivid memories of those nine days. Her little home was exactly as she had left it: the New York Times unfolded on the dining table with her magnifying glass lying upon it that morning, a tea cup and tea bag on the counter in the kitchen with a slice of lemon. The appurtenances of daily living that were unique to her—sewing, books, note cards and scratch pads, paintings, sea shells, a terra cotta sculpture of a little boy kneeling—jumped out in high relief. I fell into my mother's bed totally drained.

When I awoke the following morning I was stunned by the palpable quiet surrounding me. I experienced the same feeling each time I entered her living space during those first days and nights in Maine, and I can still sense it when I recall that time. And the sunlight! It was so bright you could practically slice it! Without her Leo energy to absorb and deflect and manage her surroundings, the sun shone almost too brightly.

Resolutions

But it was comforting, as well. I knew she was there. She was with me, and all I had to do was to take one thing at a time as she had told me only four months before.

I thought back to Sue and Laura and our final days and nights with Mary. We had empowered one another in an odyssey that was new to us all and I knew that I would need everything that we had learned. They were with me, too.

One thing at a time, Victoria had said, and my brothers and I did just that. We made the necessary calls and pulled together the final arrangements for Victoria. Her body would be cremated. "When I am gone I don't want any weeping over the body!" she had admonished. "It's just a body and I will be through with it!"

We met with the pastor at St. Duncan's Chapel in Elsworth. It was a challenging assignment, but the minister eventually agreed to the self-styled (by us) memorial service with him officiating as needed or an Episcopalian funeral service. Richard would read from the Scriptures; I would read from the writings I had brought—pieces she knew and liked—with perhaps something new; Charles would speak as well, though he did not know what he would say. We spent several days pulling everything together in a way that would work for us all and speak for her as well.

Death, I was learning, is fraught with detail, and Charles attended to the legal particulars. He filed her death certificate with the Probate Court on August 5th, her seventy-fifth birthday. The cremation was bizarre, but how could it be otherwise going through it for the first time, moreover for your mother? Her body was taken from the funeral home to a local cemetery where the procedure was performed on site. My brothers and I and my sister-in-law went together to see her for the last time on yet another shining summer morning. A brilliant sun accompanied us throughout the final odyssey of our Leo mother, and for that I was grateful. I could not have held up in the rain at that time.

It was a hands-on experience, one that I am glad to have had, but it spawned a host of off-the-wall thoughts: *What do you wear to a*

Resolutions

cremation—your mother's cremation! What do you do? Is there some sort of protocol? This was worse than attending my first funeral as a bride of three weeks. *What to do? What to say? How to be?*

In Victoria's case, I thought it would be appropriate to wear something I knew she would like so I pulled on a black T-shirt with two great blue cat eyes, a pink nose and whiskers. She loved cats. Should she be looking down on all this—and I knew that she was—she would not want us to stand on ceremony. Jeans and sandals would be fine for August in Maine. *It's not me, it's just my body.*

My brothers and sister-in-law and I rode into the shady New England cemetery. Charles parked the car, and slowly we climbed out beside a low stone building with an inordinately tall chimney. This would be the place. An attendant showed us into a room where Victoria's body lay in what appeared to be a long cardboard box set on a gurney. She was still clad in her cotton gown, a sheet folded across her legs. My most vivid remembrance is her hair waving gracefully away from her brow. It was clean and fragrant, and I ran my fingers through it as I looked down at her, my eyes filling.

My mother, my mother, my mother! I was looking into her face for the last time! As with Mary, the features were hers, but they were not *her*.

It was time for this to happen. I left the room and walked outside and sat down on the stone doorstep in the sun. The stone step was warm, and it seemed a good place to be until I heard an appalling noise that brought me to my feet. I looked up quickly and saw the great chimney spewing black smoke, and the lick of flames.

Auschwitz! Bergen-Belsen! Krakow! Mother!

I bolted from the step as if shot from a cannon and fled into the roadway that wound through the cemetery. I ran hard for as long as I could, my feet pounding the pavement until I was forced to stop and wipe my eyes. At least I was away. That felt good. I relaxed and began to walk, calmed by fresh air, and took in my surroundings.

The cemetery was a lush sanctuary, hilly

and green and shaded with ancient trees. Many of the tombstones were tall and elaborate. Some towered. Some leaned. There were simple headstones with inscriptions nearly worn away by the elements, modest headstones unobtrusive in the grass, flat stones flush with the ground. It was like something out of a Washington Irving story, pure New England.

The peace and quiet resonated like the stillness of my mother's apartment. I let the roadway take me where it would until I came to a stone bench facing a small reflecting pool. I sat down and allowed my thoughts to travel at will as the sun warmed my back. I thought of my mother's dazzling smile, my brothers, Susan— my sister-in-law—my niece and nephew. It was rather brave the way we were managing the rather hands-on odyssey of our mother's passage. I was proud of us all. Victoria would approve.

Footsteps fell behind me and a hand rested upon my shoulder. It was Charles. He lowered himself beside me on the stone bench and we sat together in silence. I turned and smiled at him. I was going to make it. We would all make it. We sat together admiring the scene, then walked back to the parking lot where Richard and Susan were waiting to drive back to Surry.

That evening our Uncle Henry flew in to Bangor from Port Washington, the perfect antidote for the day. He was one of Victoria's "little" younger brothers, as opposed to her "older" younger brothers, Bowlik and John. Henry and John were the only Polish uncles we knew at all. Both had come into our lives for extended periods when we were growing up and we adored them.

John had been our mother's favorite, a health nut and body builder decades before the fitness era, with sky blue eyes, a shock of wavy blonde hair and a laugh that defied the fates. He exuded a *joie de vivre* that we had never known, an unbridled style that was uniquely his with his blue jeans and western boots, beautiful women and shiny sports cars. He swept in and out of our lives like a comet, dazzling us with his stories and adventures, and disappeared into the West after his third divorce. No one knew how to

Resolutions

reach him. It was Henry who would come to Victoria's funeral representing the Ochenkoskis of Port Washington.

Henry had spent the winter of 1956 with our family on Silverside Road. My brothers and I did not know at the time that he was going through a painful separation and divorce, that he was losing his little boy, and that it was, in all likelihood, the darkest time of his life. We thought he was there to be our Uncle Henry, to build ice sculptures and igloos and play "Duck, Duck, Goose" in the record snow that fell on northern Delaware in the winter of 1956. He was our playmate, our comrade. I had not seen him in thirty years.

Henry's flight arrived late in the evening, and there he was the next morning sitting at Charles' and Susan's dining table with his back to the window, sunlight framing features that were unmistakably kin to Victoria. That was reason enough for wonder, but what took my attention—beyond the swarthy glow of a seaman's complexion against the aqua shirt he wore—was the masculine summation of our mother's dark eyes and brilliant smile, the shape of his forehead, his ears, his hands. I wanted to reach out and trace every feature with my finger tip, but instead I sat beside him and grinned. None of us could stop grinning. There he was, all of him. Our Uncle Henry.

The funeral was in the afternoon. Susan and I had already picked up Victoria's ashes. Rather than have them delivered by rural delivery to the Guilford's mailbox (!) we opted to pick them up ourselves, which meant returning to the cemetery office in Brewer.

It felt bizarre stepping into the stone building that I had fled a few days before. There I was standing at a counter rehearsing in my mind the words that my mouth should form. I had the sensation of being outside my body, standing to one side as this person who was me went through the motions of a transaction. Somehow the words came.

"I am here to pick up the ashes of Victoria Guilford," I heard myself say.

There. I had said it and I did not waver, but it was all I could do to remain standing when

Resolutions

a modest cardboard box was placed on the counter before me.

"Thank you," I said weakly, grasping the box with both hands and turning away before I fell completely apart. Blindly, I followed Susan to the car and slid into the front seat on the passenger side. My niece and nephew, Alice and Sam, were in the back. I held the parcel on my lap and turned toward them. Sam's great brown eyes and Alice's great blue eyes gazed back at me. *Focus on their eyes! Focus on their eyes!* I did not cry.

On the way home an interesting thing happened. In her later years, my mother would often wait in the car on days she had difficulty walking while I ran an errand.

"Now you go on, and take your time," she would say. "I am fine here." She always had something to read or something to sew, so I would take her at her word and dash off for an errand or two and find her pleasantly occupied when I returned.

On this particular day we needed to stop at the grocery. I put the cardboard box on the car seat and patted it.

"We'll be right back," I said. I looked at Susan and we both laughed. Victoria was loving it, I was sure. We picked up a few groceries and returned to the house to make lunch before the funeral service at 1 p.m.

Duncan's Chapel is a quintessential New England-style church with white clapboard and green shutters. Tall windows let in a flood of sunlight and an ample breeze. It was another stunning New England day.

Victoria's ashes had been carefully transferred from the cardboard box to a rectangular box covered with red cloth in a Chinese pattern that stood out boldly in the vestibule. Family members—my brothers and Uncle Henry, Sam and Alice and Susan and I— were seated in a front pew on the right side of the church. I was glad to be able to look outside and feel the summer air wafting through the open window.

Summer. Mother. I thought of how she looked at the ocean in Stone Harbor where our family used to spend the month of August, the favorite yellow beach umbrella that offered a fluttering reminder for children meandering in the surf of where the family was encamped and for respite from the sun. She always sat under the umbrella but managed to become deeply tanned which accentuated the dark hair and eyes and brilliant smile. That umbrella was one of her favorite things, a symbol of family times, good times, and I wondered what ever happened to it during all the moves. How sad it must have been for her to let it go…

Many people filtered into the church, all friends of Charles and Susan. Among them were several visiting Russians who were appearing in a cultural exchange with the Surry Opera Company to which Charles and Susan belonged. They came to show respect for their American hosts, and to recognize a universal loss. "When somebody's mother dies, everyone's mother dies," Charles said. Victoria would like this, too.

One at a time Charles and Richard and I rose to make a contribution to our mother's memorial. Richard read from the Scriptures and from the Episcopal Book of Common Prayer that our mother had loved. I read three poems—one for my family in Kentucky who could not be present, one that I knew that she would like, and a third that evolved while staying in her sunny apartment noting the things that were particular to who she was. It felt good reading until I looked into Uncle Henry's eyes looking up at me from the front row. *Her eyes.* The world swam as I finished reading and sat down.

Charles contributed a stirring summation, noting that Victoria had been named in honor of the end of the Great War the year she was born. He acknowledged our Russian guests and the appropriateness of their being present. Then the service ended with a rousing rendition of Amazing Grace.

A raw finality overtook me as we worked our way through all the verses. My brothers left the pew as soon as the last note filled the air. Charles led, carrying the cloth-covered Chinese box. Then Richard. With eyes brimming and spilling over, I fumbled in the pew with my papers and purse until Richard did the most touching thing. He came back for me. He turned at the door of the church, walked back to my pew, and held out his hand to me. It was the most gracious gesture, and I was utterly relieved to be helped to my feet. Arm in arm we walked down the aisle of the church out into the August sun, and into the rest of our lives.

The afternoon was a Victoria Fest. Susan loaded a picnic basket with lemonade and Toll House cookies and fruit and whatever goodies we could find from the numerous offerings of neighbors and friends, and we headed out with the red Chinese box to Sea Wall, one of Victoria's favorite spots to walk by the ocean.

It was a glorious summer afternoon. Sailboats skimmed the water, gulls dipped and dived along the surf and the ocean sparkled. We spread a blanket on the sand and enjoyed our interesting array of treats. We cast Victoria's ashes in the surf and in the tide pools and took pictures of one another and of Uncle Henry. A very Victoria day at the beach.

Uncle Henry left early the following morning. He took back with with him a tin of Victoria's ashes to scatter in Manhasset Bay off of

Barbara Victoria

Sands Point, Long Island. My brothers and I spent the next several days dismantling our mother's sunny home, sorting things for storage, things we wanted shipped, things to give away. Pictures, sewing, clothes, books, household goods. All the remnants of a life, her life. When the apartment was finally empty, vacuumed and scrubbed for inspection, our mother's home was gone and we were exhausted. It had all happened in nine days.

I flew back to Kentucky with another container of her ashes that I scattered at Ashland Gardens in Lexington, one of her favorite places to walk when she lived there. I also cast them into the pond at Basin Spring for a lover of water.

"One day you'll do this for me," I said to my son and daughter who stood on the dock with their father, watching. I took pictures of ashes wafting across the pond.

She had taken us all to places we never imagined; we returned her to the places she had visited and loved. A Polish-American girl of many homes in many destinations, always our mother.

Three months later I received a letter from

the Sparrowgrass Poetry Forum to whom I had sent the poem on a spring day after Victoria had nudged me into it. Acceptance guaranteed publication in the annual anthology, which received hundreds of submissions from across the U.S. and from seven foreign countries. There was also prize money involved for ten poets to be spread among the second and third place awards, and several honorable mentions. There was only one first prize, however. My poem had been accepted but that was not all. *Rural Perspective* won the first place award, and I received a certificate with a check for five hundred dollars. The poem would also appear on the first page of the anthology.

All of this was a thorough surprise. It was the first contest I had ever entered and I did not expect to win anything. But it paled beside the validation I had received from the Universe by way of the sometimes vanquished and always valiant Victoria. A product of her time and birth, she had forged her way with sheer will and force of character and often grace through raw fear and circumstance into a season of her own that

Barbara Victoria

finally brought her a measure of joy and peace. And, in a crowning motherly gesture, she had finally said to me, albeit indirectly, "Why not?"
Amazing grace, indeed!

Resolutions

Barbara Victoria

Resolutions

Robert

Barbara Victoria

Resolutions

1912—1992

Barbara Victoria

Resolutions

Islands in the Snow

After nineteen years,
thank you
for coming back

thank you
for eight snowy days in Maine
  you and I and
Daisy Mae and Albert
  (your Siamese sweethearts
  now mine)

for bread rising
  through us, around us, for us
chicken noodle soup simmering
cookies, cookies, cookies-
  oatmeal with raisins
    tollhouse, oatmeal again-
biscuits and cornbread,
scrapple breakfasts,

Barbara Victoria

muffins, applesauce and
submarine sandwiches (forbidden
   but relished), cold brew
sparkling wine,

for you laughing with your teeth out
   at Victor Borge on tape—
me laughing at you laughing at Victor Borge,
Borge playing Claire de Lune all the way through
   without laughing,
tears in my eyes

for another ride
through a Currier and Ives winterland
   you bundled in a mask
   oxygen in the back seat
to visit Hetty and (animal) friends
bread and cheese with Hetty
laughing with Hetty

for, "What a good meal!"
   morning, noon and night, and
"Thank you for a nice day"
   as you sat on the edge of the bed
      in your red union suit,

Resolutions

catching your breath before swinging your legs
  under the covers for the night

for eight days
to watch your face
and the sweetest blue eyes
  this side of Paradise,
to witness
what intrigued you, what made you laugh,
what made you angry
the things you love —
cats
snow
a new cap, warm socks
suspenders
children getting off the school bus
a green thumb for strawberry begonias
pictures of grandchildren, pictures of family,
pictures of friends
the "sexiest dance" (your words)
                    from The Sound of Music *—*
  a romantic waltz (mine) —
Peter Paul and Mary singing Puff the Magic Dragon
  and Blowin' in the Wind,
thank you for Burl Ives ballads

Barbara Victoria

which I had not heard since you sang them last
    on the road to Grandma and Grandpa's
Harry Belafonte
watercolors
being a grandfather
cats, cats,
cats.

Thank you for coming back
for eight snowy days, in time
for me to be your daughter
always!

Resolutions

Barbara Victoria

Resolutions

Robert Hendryx Guilford was born in Cleveland, in Ohio, on Friday the Thirteenth in September of 1912. His father, Charles MacNeal, or "Mac," was the first generation to leave the family farm in upstate New York and seek a living outside the dairy business. He worked in sales for a New York haberdasher and spent a lot of time on the road, which left his only son as the man of the house for older sister, Beulah, younger sister, Ruth, and his mother, Irene Hendryx Guilford.

The family lived in Port Washington, Long Island, on Bar Beach Road when Robert met my mother. I do not know how long they

Barbara Victoria

courted, but they married on the second day of September in 1939. A wedding picture was taken outside the church after the ceremony. My parents and grandparents are wearing dark clothing, my mother in a brown suit, her rich, dark hair rolled under a stylish hat and veil, Robert in a dark suit and fedora. Mac looks appropriately distinguished. My grandmother, Irene Hendryx Guilford, is dressed in black. It was not considered good luck to wear black to weddings in those days, but Irene chose black for the marriage of her only son, and this was not lost upon her new daughter-in-law. The group is basically congenial looking, however. The world lay before the young couple in 1939, and the popular song *Somewhere Over the Rainbow* from the hit movie *The Wizard of Oz* became their signature.

My mother's smile dazzles in the wedding photograph, but my favorite picture of my father is not from that day. It was taken in the backyard of the house on Bar Beach Road. He is strolling in the grass, dressed in wool slacks, a V-neck sweater with a white shirt open at the neck, and casual shoes. The sun plays upon a shock of fair hair that is neatly parted and combed to one side. He has turned to acknowledge a black dachshund that has run up beside him in the grass, and he is about to bend down. A trim and elegant figure, he could pass for a royal cousin of Edward VIII. No wonder he swept Victoria away.

Robert had aspired to follow his grandfather, Coy Hendryx, into law, but the Great Depression intervened. He was forced to drop out of Colgate University after two years and, upon the advice of his mother, trained to become a court reporter. There was good money in it, Irene had advised, and she proved to be right. He perfected Pitman shorthand taking 225 words per minute with a dip pen, and landed a job with the Court of Chancery in Wilmington, Delaware, where he and Victoria moved and began raising a family. Because Delaware has no corporation tax, the Court of Chancery received lucrative cases from around the country and overseas, and Robert was able to afford the family a comfortable living. In time, the pre-fab Gunnison home nestled into five acres on

Barbara Victoria

Silverside Road would be sold for a color-coordinated Cape Cod in the burgeoning subdivision of Faulk Woods, a summer cottage in Lewes... He was the quintessential "good provider," as my mother liked to put it.

Robert and a colleague were sought after for lengthy trials in the Court of Chancery as the only two court reporters in the state of Delaware who could transcribe one another's shorthand. Robert was highly respected around the Court; however, something basic was thwarted in him by his work. His grandfather had been a lawyer in upstate New York and an uncle had been a judge in Michigan. Transcribing a hand-penned transcript and reading it into a dictaphone must have been equivalent to serving as a secretary when your heart and mind are programmed to be the CEO. A good court reporter has to turn themself off to become a conduit for words—the words of others—and to transform them onto paper and into court record. Perhaps this exercise generated a restlessness in him, the mental acuity needing to be engaged, a spirit thwarted, but he was a prime target for L. Ron Hubbard and the Church of Scientology when he read the first book on Dianetics in 1952. Scientology turned him on, and thereafter he poured considerable time and resources into Hubbard's enterprises in an association that became lifelong.

In an effort to reconcile her husband's passion for Scientology with the life of her family, my mother became as active in the Church of Scientology as her already full agenda would allow between scouting and spearheading the UNICEF fund drive, and other volunteer enterprises. There were trips to Washingon, D.C. to conventions and meetings. Robert invited some of his new colleagues to the house on Silverside Road. But after several years Victoria withdrew from it all and poured her energies into her family and community work. In retrospect she would say that Scientology caused the divorce, but I would have to say that I know better. Robert and Victoria were too disparate in background and temperament to meld indefinitely. Robert was a far cry from the rough and tumble of the Ochenkoski brothers, and Victoria might have thrived with someone more demonstrative than my father's nature would allow. While Robert responded to a personality with his mother's managerial directive, I believe he needed a gentler temperament than his wife could sustain.

Within this context the marriage snapped. My brother, Richard, was a principal casualty, suffering a nervous breakdown in the spring of his senior year of high school that thrust him in and out of mental hospitals for the next year— and periodically for years to come. He was diagnosed as schizophrenic, later as bi-polar with schizophrenic features. My father would have nothing to do with psychiatry, opting instead for the methods of Scientology to approach the son who, in fact, seemed more like him than his other children. My mother was desperate for solutions, caught between her son and his father as Richard careened from one treatment to another.

I remember the night that my father left the house in Faulk Woods. Robert had a taste for dry martinis, but that night he was having vodka. He was sitting in the breakfast "nook," as it was termed in those days, where, to my unending

Resolutions

fascination, the checkered curtains matched the checkered wallpaper. Perhaps a standard blowup had occurred between them or maybe this one was specific to time and resources being poured into Scientology, but the next thing I knew my mother had hurled a nearly empty vodka bottle, hitting my father in the forehead. It barely broke the skin, but his soul was rent, and at age sixteen I knew it. The blue eyes were stunned and abashed. He tried to mask his hurt and humiliation, pausing to compose himself at the table. Then he rose quietly and withdrew to their bedroom where he began removing his things from the closet. I do not know where he went that night. I don't remember anything at all until I visited him for the first time in a high-rise apartment weeks later in downtown Wilmington. One familiar piece of furniture in the sparsely furnished room, a ladder-back chair with a split-oak seat, had been in the Guilford family. Victoria had thought he should have it. Other than that he was on his own.

It took two years for the divorce to become final in the state of Delaware. In the

Barbara Victoria

meantime, Robert lived spartanly, dressed well, and drove a cream-colored Porsche which he enjoyed taking to weekend gymkhanas. Janet Tucker, a fellow Scientologist, eventually moved into the high-rise apartment with him, and they were married three weeks after his divorce was final. Richard served as best man.

The last time I saw much of Robert was 1964 between my freshman and sophomore years of college. The highlight of that summer was the two of us driving in the Porsche to visit his youngest sister, Ruth, in Hatboro, Pennsylvania, where my grandparents were visiting as well. I had not seen them all since well before the divorce. Mac, as my grandfather was called (but not by his grandchildren!), was in the advanced stages of Alzheimer's disease, and the once gruff exterior had dissolved into childlike sweetness. I was glad to witness the interior of him, and was profoundly touched. It was the last time I would see my grandparents alive, and the last I would see of my father for nineteen years. I was nineteen years old.

After Robert and Janet married, I have to

Resolutions

assume that they become more deeply involved in Scientology. He left his job with the Court of Chancery after twenty-three years, just two years short of full retirement. He and Janet lived and worked on a ship with L. Ron Hubbard and Co. that cruised the Mediterranean for eight years.

I sent him a letter with the pictures of his first grandchild through a stateside address just after my daughter was born, but it was returned three months later. After that he was lost to me, and I began raising a daughter and then a son without discussing their Guilford grandfather at all. I did not know how to talk about him with my children, how to explain where he was or why I did not know. I didn't know myself. It seemed too much for young hearts and minds to handle, and it was certainly too much for mine, so I set it aside for a time when they were older to begin unraveling the Gordian knot of the Guilford family.

Fast forward to Christmas of 1982 at Basin Spring Farm in central Kentucky. My brother, Charles, is coming from Maine, and Richard and our mother are coming from Virginia, and

Barbara Victoria

Lexington, Kentucky, respectively. Enroute, Charles stops in Washington, D.C., and makes inquiries at the "Org"—Scientology for the national "organization"—as to the whereabouts of Robert Guilford and learns that he is living in Miami, Florida. The day after Christmas he pipes up in front of the extended family gathering, "Let's call Daddy."

"Daddy?" *What?* He had long ago ceased being "Daddy" to me. "Daddys" don't go away for years at a time, decades.

Why this, why now? I wondered. I was utterly stunned. That is how my daughter and son learned about their Guilford grandfather. We made the call and all talked with him on the phone.

"Hello, uh … Daddy?" The conversation on my part started out haltingly but we were soon carrying on as if we called one another every weekend. Robert had never met his son-in-law; he did not know of his granddaughter and grandson; he had not talked with any of us for years, and there we were, gabbing away. It was pleasant, nice, intriguing; I was glad that he was

well and happy. But afterwards I did not feel particularly connected or moved to maintain an ongoing relationship. I could take it or leave it.

My ten-year-old daughter, Tessa, felt otherwise. She was infatuated with the idea of having another grandfather—after all, she had always known two grandmothers—and she wanted to know him and for him to know her. So with ten-year-old innocence and enthusiasm she wrote an "I am Tessa" letter to her newfound grandfather telling him about her school and her friends and what she liked to do. She put in a school picture as well. Then she asked me to mail the letter for her.

I was utterly terrified. *What if he doesn't answer? What if SILENCE is her answer?*

I could not bear for her to go through the "Big No," and I could not bear it myself. Not again. So I carried the letter in my purse to think about it. I carried it for three weeks.

Finally my husband said, "You have no right to do that." *Whoa!*

"And you have no idea what it is like to go through what I have," I shot back.

Barbara Victoria

True, he could not know, but after thinking about it for a day or two I knew he was right. It wasn't my call. Finally, I put a stamp on my daughter's letter and dropped into a mailbox in Hardinsburg. I couldn't mail it from home where it would lie for half a day. It had to be done where I could not change my mind.

I can hardly imagine what it must have been like for him to receive a letter from the little girl in Kentucky who was his granddaughter. All I know is that six weeks went by before a letter arrived from Miami. Six long weeks. Thus began a gentle correspondence, however, through which my daughter began to know her grandfather, and I began to know my father again.

It was to Tessa that Robert said in one of his letters, "Why don't you ask your mother what she would think if we (Janet and I) came for a visit?"

They arrived the following June, in time for my thirty-eighth birthday. Janet's nephew in Ohio was getting married, and Robert and Janet had bought a new little Ford Escort for the trip. They were coming to see us along the way.

Resolutions

We were eating a spring supper of fresh greens from the garden when they pulled into the driveway at Basin Spring Farm. I realized later that I literally had spinach on my teeth as I greeted my father for the first time in nineteen years, though he kindly said nothing. It was nicely ironic, but he was no doubt too stunned to notice. Here was a thoroughly grown daughter, a son-in-law, and a granddaughter and grandson living on a rolling farm in Central Kentucky. I am sure it was overwhelming, to say the least.

The integration of that visit into both our lives is the most stunning amalgamation I have ever engineered. I knew that, given the enormity of it all, either of us could stumble, perhaps fatally for our relationship, and I did not want that to happen. He made a couple of attempts to explain what caused the disconnect here or there because of what was happening in his life at that time. But I knew—and I believe he did as well—that the exercise was patently absurd. What mattered was that we were together on a shining day in June. It mattered that he had finally met his son-in-law, the ten-year-old granddaughter

Barbara Victoria

who had written to him and without whom he would not be there, and the eight-year-old grandson who led him to the spring to see two raccoons treed by the family dog. Nineteen years had been lost to my father and I, but we had stepped together into present time. That was all that mattered.

It was a watershed time. After he and Janet made their way to Ohio and back to Florida, however, I found myself slipping back into a casual feeling about him. We had a pleasant enough association, but frankly I could take it or leave it. I did travel to Florida over another birthday to help him and Janet pack for their move to Maine. Charles had married and had a family, and our mother had moved there six months earlier to live in a retirement facility similar to the one where Janet and Robert had placed their names on a waiting list. It happened very quickly. And as I began visiting them all in Maine, Robert and I really discovered one another again. I realized that we had a similar sense of humor, that we shared a playful irreverence, that we had similar feet and toes...

Resolutions

Janet died eight months into their first year at Bullfrog Junction, and the next time I saw my father he was a widower. He enjoyed showing me around, however, and we took an unforgettable drive through Currier and Ives country on a snow-laden November afternoon. On my following visit I celebrated another birthday with him at an oyster bar in Castine. By then he had met Hetty, who was probably the match of his life. They were both too far along in years and deteriorating health for anything as formal as marriage—my father with emphysema and Hetty with advancing sclera derma, a debilitating disease of the immune system. But theirs was a jolly and a tender association.

On days when they were both physically challenged, they would talk on the phone, sometimes several times, laughing about their infirmities. On good days they would spring free in the Ford Escort for excursions along the Maine coastline or into the countryside poking into art galleries or to attend a local concert of chamber music or poetry reading—whatever happened to be going on at the time. It was a gifted

Barbara Victoria

partnership, and my appreciation of its genius drew my father and me together. His ready sense of humor, wide-ranging tastes and dapper style made it understandable that he would attract someone like Hetty, a vivid writer who ran an art gallery in the front of her little house, and composted a garden in the backyard. I relished them together.

Robert enjoyed several good years watching my niece and nephew toddle from babyhood into childhood. In early January of 1992, however, he was admitted to the hospital, with severe breathing problems that led to respiratory failure. It was a horrific scare all the way around and he vowed to never go through it again. He came home to recuperate, was readmitted to the hospital, came home, and was readmitted again in a span of weeks. By the end of January my brother and my father were wearing down, so I flew to Maine to help with next steps, getting him home again and operational with home care.

I was determined to make the most of my time with him, not knowing how much we would have. And I wanted to spoil him. So I packed a medium-sized pot into a string bag for simmering nourishing soups and broths, a rolling pin to bake his favorite homemade bread, and a few other kitchen items that were key to my mission. It was going to be a *tour de force. Yes!*

Charles picked me up at the airport and we went straight to the hospital where we found our father propped up on pillows, looking out an expanse of windows at the ice heaves clamoring for the shoreline of Morgan Bay. It was bitter cold in the dead of winter on the coastline of southeastern Maine.

He gave us a big smile, and we visited until it was confirmed that he would not be released that day. There was plenty for me to do, however, and I told him I would be back later. He gave me the keys to his apartment. Charles and I drove to his work and he handed me the keys to his car. The *tour de force* was about to commence.

Ironically, after my mother died, my father moved into the same retirement complex

Barbara Victoria

that she had lived in, only a couple of units down. His unit was on the very end of the row close to a pine woods which gave it a feeling of privacy. Driving by her apartment for the first time since her death was a daunting proposition, and I braced myself. On a subsequent trip, however, I had to pull over as my eyes overflowed. To my utter astonishment a woman about my mother's age, who looked enough like Victoria to be her—haircut, glasses and all—held the door open as a little boy came running up the walkway. It could have been my nephew, Sam, arriving at apartment G-4, running into his Grandmother Vicky's arms for an afternoon of stories or to take an interesting walk along Morgan Bay. *Whew!* I lost it.

I let myself into my father's apartment and I found myself looking at the same layout as my mother's, only in reverse. The only thing to do was to keep moving. I changed the bed, scrubbed floors, vacuumed and dusted between loading the washer and drier in the laundry room at the other end of the complex. Later that evening I returned to the hospital to visit my

father who brightly reported that he would be released the following morning. *All right!*

We reached his apartment before noon the next day and it did not take long to get him settled. He was overjoyed to see his Siamese cats, Albert and Daisy Mae, who proceeded to curl up with him —one on his lap and the other on the back of his easy chair. After he dozed off, I grabbed my grocery list and dashed for the door. I was possessed with the idea of having his little home awash with the fragrance of home cooking as soon as he awoke.

In the interest of time, I stopped at a small grocery in Blue Hill that looked as though it could cover the basics. It was a real Mom and Pop operation with creaky wooden floors that made a modern grocery cart bump over old planks polished by years of footwear.

I had never cooked for my father, so I picked out things I thought he would like, things that I knew would be good for him, and things that I enjoyed making. For starters, an assortment of fruit, including bananas, and apples to eat whole or to make into applesauce.

Barbara Victoria

I picked up a bag of whole wheat flour for bread and muffins and whole wheat pancakes, raisins for the muffins, baker's yeast for the bread, unbleached flour for biscuits, scrapple which I knew he loved, plus eggs, milk, juice, instant pudding, chocolate chips and brown sugar for Toll House cookies. I dashed along the aisles, my eyes welling over, and I had to stop to wipe them to make out my handwriting and to see where I was going.

How is he doing? Is he awake yet?

I didn't want him to find himself alone, I didn't want him to be scared, I didn't want him to be sad... Hurrying down my list, I picked out a small chicken to simmer for soup, plus egg noodles, celery, carrots and onions. I had to stop to clear my eyes again and again.

Tour de force. Tour de force. Tour de force! Come on, girl!

When I returned to the apartment he was still dozing with Albert and Daisy Mae. *Whew!* I tried to be ever-so-quiet, but he began to stir as I unpacked the grocery bags.

"Thought I'd make us some chicken

noodle soup," I called out casually, as though it was utterly commonplace. "How does that sound?"

"That would be just fine, honey, whatever you want to make," he said, as he stroked Daisy Mae on his lap.

Chicken noodle soup it was, steaming and fragrant, and hot biscuits with butter and honey, with fruit cocktail for dessert. He ate well. I cleaned up the kitchen while he got ready for bed. After taking out his false teeth for the night he sat on the edge of the bed in his red union suit and looked up at me with marble blue eyes.

"Thank you for such a nice day," he said, with a toothless smile.

"And thank *you* for such a nice day," I replied, hugging him, and tucked him in as Daisy Mae and Albert joined him for the night.

I turned out the light and tiptoed out into the living room where I sank into a chair. It had been a long day, but everything had gone like clockwork. We had a lot of loose ends to pull together, but we were on our way. We were home. We had plenty of food laid in for the week. And we had one another's undivided attention for the first time in my adult life. *Tour de force, indeed.*

The next morning I fixed a breakfast of scrapple, scrambled eggs, bran muffins with raisins, juice and coffee. We talked for a while as we sipped our coffee. The conversation came around to his time in the Mediterranean with L. Ron Hubbard, and what that had been like.

"I haven't been a very good father," he said, looking at me with those blue eyes.

"That's not true," I replied, putting my hand on his. "You were the father I chose, and you were the father I needed in order to become who I am." *How can there be anything wrong with where we are? All is as it is meant to be!*

In the years since 1983 when I had begun to know him, I had one recurring problem: I did not know what to call him. "Daddy" just didn't work any more. "Robert" felt more authentic and I had been calling him that, which he didn't mind—I believe he was glad to be called anything—but "Robert" seemed too trendy. On this visit I began to call him "Dad." It felt right. *Dad. Yes!*

Resolutions

Our days were full as I cooked and puttered about his little home. I loved doing things for him! Charles and Susan would stop by or bring Sam and Alice to see their grandfather. A home health nurse came by and instructed us about his medications. He was taking seven different prescriptions and three inhalers—many at different times. It was all very confusing, so I mapped out a schedule on paper that would help us remember it all. We arranged for someone to come by and straighten and clean for him. I helped him write out checks for his bills one morning when, due to his many medications, he simply could not remember what he was doing to complete the task. He became very distraught.

"Oh, let me. It won't take us long to do it together," I said breezily, and we talked about this and that while I wrote them out.

One day Hetty came by and I fixed lunch for us all. Another day we loaded his oxygen tank into the back seat of the Escort and drove through the snowy landscape to have lunch with her in her cozy little New England home. He tired quickly and we couldn't stay long, but it was a convivial time and that was good.

In the evening we would watch the news while enjoying a beer together—he had always relished a cold beer. Then we would watch *M.A.S.H.* reruns or pop in one of his videotapes of Victor Borge in concert, or Peter Paul and Mary. One night we watched *The Sound of Music*, one of his favorite films.

Later in the week we were snowed in and watched in fascination as snow whirled around the corner windows of the nook where he sat in his blue easy chair with Albert and Daisy Mae. We were lost to the world and it was just fine. There was plenty of food. We had one another, we had the cats—or, rather, the cats had us! When the snow stopped and there had been time for roads to be plowed (Mainers are great about that!) I loaded his oxygen tank into the back seat of the Ford Escort once more, and we went for another Currier and Ives excursion. Returning to the house he slipped on some ice at the front door and both of us went down. At first I was stunned, and then swept with fear that he had broken something. He was embarrassed and full of

Resolutions

apology, but soon we were both laughing as we climbed to our feet.

I tucked him into his easy chair with a blanket when we got inside and sat down beside his footstool. The afternoon sun shone through the windows on us as I laid my head on his knee.

"I've got my golden girl back," he said softly, stroking my hair with his beautiful tapered hands. I was glad he could not see my face. *Yes, Yes,* I thought as tears crawled down my cheeks. We were right where we needed to be. At last I was able to be the daughter that I wanted to be to him.

Richard arrived from Virginia late in the week and began spending time with us. Richard the Lion Hearted, as we had called him, was a bachelor working at a blue-collar job in a construction business where his attention to detail was engaged managing the parts department. He would always be on medication, but he had friends who looked out for him at work, and friends in the Episcopal church where he sang in the choir and served as a lay reader.

Our logistical work complete, all we

needed to do was to be together. Charles and his family were in and out, and Richard and Dad visited with one another. We were all a family again.

The night before my flight back to Kentucky I began coming down with something. My throat ached, my head hurt. But we were having a "family meeting." Dad had called my brothers and me together to talk about practicalities after he was gone. We ordered in pizzas, and Susan and Sam and Alice joined us for dinner.

After supper, Susan took the children home and we began digging into the issues that lay before us. Taking care of "business" was one thing. The awful part was slipping back into traditional sibling roles.

"As the eldest, Charles will be executor..." our father intoned, and then said something about the "family mantle." Richard and I glanced at one another. We had always occupied the low rungs of the family totem pole and had just been reminded of it. After the days we had just shared I could not

Resolutions

believe this was happening, but I did what I had always done: I kept quiet and waited for it to end.

My head was pounding and my throat ached. I was in the grip of something nasty and was terrified that my father might catch it. In his condition he could not weather the least bit of congestion, let alone a full-blown chest cold or a sinus infection. Or—God forbid—the flu!

After my brothers left I tucked my father into bed one last time.

"Thank you for another nice day," he said, as he had every night I had been with him.

"And thank *you* for such a nice day," I replied, hugging his thin frame. It was nice to be back to just the two of us.

I collapsed into the daybed out in the living room, my head reeling, and it was a long time before I fell asleep.

Don't let him get this! I've got to get away before he catches anything! He was so vulnerable physically, and on so many medications. It would be the end for him.

I awoke just before the sun began filtering through the pine woods.

Barbara Victoria

How can I possibly leave him! In all likelihood it was the last time I would see my father alive. If I knew it then he knew it, too.

How are either of us going to do this!

I thought of the days we had shared, the evenings. I had prepared enough food to last him for a while, and had frozen other things to keep him well stocked. But he would be by himself most of the time.

I don't want him to feel alone, I don't want him to be afraid, and I don't want him to be sad.

To divert my swirling thoughts I began rummaging through my briefcase for my journal, and came upon a red folder. It had two handy pockets inside and three brass binder tabs down the middle. In a flash I knew how to continue putting one foot in front of the other.

A journal—Yes! We could write to one another whenever we had something to say—jot things down as though we were visiting the way we had for the last eight days. It would be an ongoing dialogue, only on paper, something to put in the mail every day or several times a week or whenever we felt like it. It would just be a different way of talking. We wouldn't be apart after all!

I wrote out our first "conversation" for him to read after I left. I could barely see through blurry eyes to finish it, but I knew this was the only way I could do it. I ended my entry with, *"I love you every day and every night, beyond all days and nights,"* and inserted it with plenty of extra paper into the tabs. *This would work, Yes! It would work for both of us.* I found some red heart stickers in my briefcase and placed one in the middle of the outside cover. *There!*

Over breakfast I explained our new "system" to my father and he liked it. Of course, we would call one another, but this would take care of those moments when you needed to say something, times when we might have called out to one another in the next room to say this or that. *We can do this. We can make it work, one day at a time! That is all any of us have.*

Charles drove me to the airport in Bangor. I was feeling horrible when I boarded the plane with my briefcase and string bag, and I curled up

Barbara Victoria

in a seat next to the window. I slept fitfully but soundly enough to miss deplaning in Boston to catch my connecting flight. By the time I was fully awake again I could hear two women in the seats ahead of me discussing their agenda in Florida. The plane was enroute to Tampa! What horror!

The rest of the flight was interminable. I arrived in Tampa at the same time my husband and son were watching passengers deplane from the flight arriving from Boston in Louisville, Kentucky. I must have been quite a sight in my winter coat and boots, soup pot and rolling pin in the string bag in one hand, briefcase in the other. I had left the snowscape of eastern Maine ten hours before and was looking at palm trees at the other end of the eastern seaboard. It was wholly absurd! And I was sick and falling apart.

Bless the Delta personnel! They scooped me up and took care of notifying the terminal in Louisville that I would be in on the last flight of the evening in Louisville at 1:15 a.m. I had a couple of hours to wait and had books to read and work to occupy me. But what I really needed to do was to call my father. He was waiting to hear that I had gotten home safely and I didn't want him to worry, but what was I going to say to him?! Oh, well, it might give us a good laugh…

I bit the bullet and dialed the phone. When I was able to get through to Maine he said he had been feeling blue and was glad to hear my voice. Then I told him where I was and he broke up. We were both laughing our insides out. The wait in the airport wasn't as long after that.

My husband and son were grinning wickedly as I reeled down the ramp at 1:15 a.m. By that time I was too sick and tired to be amused. I had exhausted every resource I had within me in eight days and eight nights. But I had been there when it mattered. I had accomplished everything I knew to do and more than a few things I didn't know to do. The *tour de force* had been realized. My father and I had been islands in the snow. I knew I would not change a thing if I did it all again, even the delirious trip to Tampa.

We wrote back and forth as we said we would. I was determined to fill his folder, and wrote whenever the spirit moved me. Sometimes it was an entire letter ready to mail. Sometimes it was a few lines or paragraphs which I added to until I had filled the front and back of a notebook page. It kept him close to me and I hoped it kept me close to him.

For the next several weeks he fell into the routine we had established. Home health nurses and aides made their rounds, and my brother and sister-in-law checked in on him as usual. Five weeks after I left Maine, however, he was back in the hospital again. It was Sunday afternoon on the first of March when my brother called. It didn't look serious, but something within the medications he was taking was either conflicting or was giving him side effects, or both. The doctor wanted to monitor him for a few days to find out how to get his system back in sync.

Perhaps it was the fresh memory of respiratory failure that haunted him, or the prospect of returning home with yet another routine, but the following morning Robert had a frank talk with his physician.

"Is this the way it is going to be, Doc,

going in and out of the hospital, going back and forth with all this medication, and tests and more tests?" he asked. "Is this what I have to look forward to?"

The heart/lung complications for which he was being treated were medically enmeshed. Treatment for one could interfere with treatment for the other. Then there were side effects from any or all of his medications, which had to be countered as well. An intricate chemical soup was keeping him alive.

"Mr. Guilford, I am afraid it is," the doctor replied.

My father then made a decision that would change all our lives. He told his doctor that he had had enough. He was foregoing further medication but he had many questions.

"What can I expect?" he asked his physician.

He was advised that the end could come within days with nothing to regulate the heart and lung functions. Robert said that he would go with it, but he wanted to remain in the hospital. This reversal of the Hippocratic oath put the hospital in the stunning position of allowing an old man to die in their midst. Requisite

Barbara Victoria

formalities were addressed, however, and he was allowed to stay.

My brother called me with news of our father's decision on a particularly busy day at the beginning of a particularly stressful week at work. Robert had embraced his own death and that was his final decision. He was purely relieved, but it was quite a bolt of news to receive on a Monday morning at the office.

I hung up the phone and sat at my desk shaking. Then I did the only thing I knew to do: I dialed a florist.

Years before, after going through surgery for the first time, my mother had sent me an arrangement of pink carnations and baby's breath that had turned into enormous company during the sleepless nights that followed. I knew the company of flowers, and explained to the woman on the other end of the phone what was taking place in Maine. Remembering *Somewhere Over the Rainbow* I asked her to send a bouquet of cut flowers, all colors, with a card that read: "*A rainbow for you, Dad! I am with you, always! Your loving Daughter.*" I hung up the phone and

Resolutions

broke down.

It was a long week. My office was being moved to another building and it was enormous work, but the physical activity was beneficial. Morning and afternoon, I would call Charles at the hospital in Maine where he remained with our father.

"What you are doing is the greatest gift you can give someone," I told him. "Pay attention. It is a lot of work, but there is everything to be learned! "

After his initial decision, Robert was euphoric. He had taken control of his life, albeit a shortened one. On Tuesday he was especially chipper, telling the nurses how pretty they looked and what a good job they were doing. We talked several times during those first two days. By Wednesday, however, he said, "...the fog is beginning to come in." It was the last time that I heard him speak. By the end of the week he had slipped into a sleep state and was no longer taking food and drink. It would not be long. I was worn out for my father and for my brother.

Driving home from work on Friday

afternoon was bittersweet. It was one of those late winter days laced with spring-to-come that can bless the Ohio Valley in February and early March. A thundershower had swept through that afternoon and the sky was blue-black. As I drove west on U.S. 60 the sun broke through the edges of a cloudbank, creating a blinding pattern of silver and illuminating the burgeoning green countryside.

It would be a beautiful day to let go, I thought to myself. *Yes! Yes!* I heard from months before. Tears were running down my cheeks.

When I arrived at the farm I went indoors to change clothes and poured myself a drink before heading back out into the yard. The sun was out again, though droplets were still falling. There might be a rainbow…

I walked out into the wet grass, taking in the fragrance of the cleansed landscape as my eyes swept the horizon. The sky was clearing, except for a bank of blue-black clouds piled against the horizon and high into the sky beyond the road that ran beside the farm. Movement caught my eye, and I saw my seventeen-year-old son loping his mare up the road toward Bewleyville. The sun illuminated the mare's copper color that shone like a new penny. I waved and Gerard waved back. Behind them a band of color descended from the clouds shining with perfect clarity against the gunmetal canopy. A perfect rainbow due Northeast. Maine!

Hearing is the last faculty to go.

I dashed into the house and dialed the hospital. Charles answered and I told him what I had just witnessed. "Put the phone to his ear," I said.

"Dad," I exclaimed, "I just saw the most stunning rainbow! Gerard was riding his mare up the road and a rainbow was shining in the sky behind him due Northeast. A rainbow for you, Dad!"

I love you every day and every night, beyond all days and nights, were the last words I spoke to my father. It was ten minutes after six Central Standard Time when I hung up the phone and raced back out into the yard. The sky had changed and the rainbow was gone.

Around twenty after eight the phone rang

Barbara Victoria

and it was Charles. Our father had drawn his last breath ten minutes before. I knew in an instant that the rainbow had been from him. It was the sixth day of March 1992, the fifth day since he had refused his medications, seven months after Victoria died, and one week short of a year since Mary had passed away.

I did not return to Maine. Robert had not wanted a funeral. At the hospital, Charles had eased our father's body into his clothes—including the Santa Claus suspenders and reindeer socks that I had given him for Christmas that had delighted the nurses—and his body was cremated. Charles contacted the Church of Scientology, and forwarded many of our father's books and papers at their request to the headquarters in Miami. Robert had been highly regarded, and a memorial service of some kind was conducted by those who had known and worked with him there.

Charles also did the kindest thing: he sent me our father's hooded winter coat, a rag wool cardigan, and a summer jacket that I wear to this day, along with some other mementos. What a

Resolutions

heroic job my brother had accomplished helping our father out of his life, gathering up what was left behind.

There was more. Several weeks passed by when a small package arrived in the mail. Inside I found a perfectly crafted wooden box with a note from Charles. He had made the box for the occasion, he said, exquisitely fashioned with the eye and hand of a master carpenter. I slid back the perfectly fitting lid and found a plastic bag containing ashes from our father's remains.

It may have been that very day or it may have been later, I do not remember, but one shining Saturday morning after a late winter snow had blanketed the farm, I trekked to the spring with the beautiful wooden box. The smooth motion was satisfying as I slid back the lid and removed the plastic bag. Around the base of the trees where Robert Hendryx Guilford and his newly acquainted grandson had admired a pair of raccoons nine years before, I scattered his ashes in the sparkling snow. I scattered them along the spring bank on the western slope of the pond. I scattered them in the woods.

Barbara Victoria

It was a dazzling winter morning. I took pictures.

Resolutions

Barbara Victoria

Resolutions

Barbara Victoria

Barbara Victoria

Resolutions

Resurrection

Out of ice
  water rushing over stone

Out of fire
  another winking constellation

Out of ash
  grasses waving in the light

Out of darkness
  a fresh path

Out of history
  a new world.

Barbara Victoria

Resolutions

They are gone—my mother, my father, my mother-in-law and friend. They are gone but I am not abandoned. Each bestowed a parting gift in the year that spanned 1991-92 that continues to resonate with all of life and eternity. Each gift offered resolution serving as a foundation for the next, and each has caused me to live differently in the years that have elapsed since that watershed time.

Much has changed. I am no longer living at Basin Spring Farm in central Kentucky. I have been divorced, left my government job at Fort Knox, and, a couple of years ago headed West where I landed in the Rocky Mountain region. On the first day of the year 2000 I married again and now live fifty miles east of Yellowstone National Park in Cody, Wyoming.

There have been other losses. Loved ones of thirty years have slipped away, casualties of divorce. The man who was my father-in-law was one until he died in a nursing home in Brandenburg, Kentucky. Our distance from one another was the saddest of losses, this man who had been a father to me for most of thirty years.

It was a protracted and difficult passage, often fraught with acrimony and convolution for the family. There were switchbacks of home care and outpatient care and hospital care and, ultimately, three years of nursing home care. He never surpassed his utter disbelief that Mary— five years his junior, and, moreover, his caretaker—would go before him. Ninety-percent deaf for most of his adult life, he felt very alone and was often scared living in the home they built in the last two decades of their life together. He was greatly loved by attentive children and grandchildren and a cadre of caretakers, but nothing they would do could assuage his anger or

Resolutions

his despair.

It wasn't supposed to be this way! How could she have done this to him?

He did not plan for an estate. He wanted only to use up his resources and die. But life went on and on in spite of emphysema and diabetes and congestive heart disease. It took a full decade for his great constitution to erode. A difficult passage, indeed.

There have been blessings, however, and loved ones who have not slipped away. I cherish an ongoing bond with my former husband and with Basin Spring Farm where I invested my youth and the childhoods of our daughter and son who are now grown. They have made us grandparents of a little girl and two little boys, much to my utter amazement and sheer wonder. *Me, a grandmother!* My former husband has married a lovely woman who has become a dear friend. And my family has been extended and enhanced with my now-husband's son and two daughters and their families, including two young grandsons. They are all my "angel children."

Barbara Victoria

Great loss, great gain, and many, many blessings. All are tempered, however, by a perspective wrought in the year of three transitions by loved ones whose final gifts are now woven into the fabric of who I am.

Mother Mary. Her transition made me a student of passage once again but in a wholly new arena. All that I had learned nearly two decades before in Lamaze classes preparing for the births of two children came rushing back with her passage. The physicality of the processes is different, the emotional nuances driven from a different place, but there is a tangible progression at the beginning and at the end of life where destiny awaits resolution.

Lamaze offers a course in birth physicality. A registered nurse had coached our class in the physical stages of early labor, active labor, transition, and the process of literally pushing the baby into the world. Each contraction is preceded by a cleansing breath followed by patterned, paced breathing particular to each stage. We learned to hold a focal point during contraction, and the benefit of

Resolutions

"effleurage," the relaxation technique of lightly massaging the abdomen, a basic and effective distraction." We learned to take a final cleansing breath punctuating the end of each contraction with the confirmation.

It is over, I can relax now. I can do this.

Physical labor is an external exercise. We were also coached on the internal progression of birth, how we could expect to feel during each stage of the work of bringing a baby into the world. Early labor is a time of confidence and optimism as breathing and rhythm are established.

This is finally it, the baby is coming!

Advanced labor calls for concentration and working partnership between the mother and the birth partner. During transition—the final stage of labor before crowning of the baby's head—we should expect a roller coaster ride driven by a gamut of emotions. The mother might feel and say anything at this time, we were advised, and birthing partners should not be alarmed by any of this but stay calm and be reassuring.

Barbara Victoria

Transition is the most telling aspect of birth. Just when you think that things cannot get any worse, when you have had all that you can stand and want only to be done with it all, you are on the precipice of a miracle: *a new life is about to enter the world!*

This awareness is central to life itself. Just at the moment of pure physical and emotional chaos, life is about to get as good as it can. This was, for me, the principle lesson of birth, one of the singular truths of this lifetime that would greet me again in the final days and hours of Mary's transition.

Hospice teaches the "Lamaze" of dying. That is where a light went on for me. It made perfect sense that if there is a physical and emotional progression for our way into the earth plane, it would be the same for the way out. *Bingo.* If I could handle one, I could handle the other. It was all do-able.

Hospice taught the physical progression and the emotional nuances that accompany the shutting down of the physical body. Lamaze in reverse! The nurse reassured us every step of the

Resolutions

way—just like a Lamaze nurse—when Mary talked "out of her head," thrashed about, gradually became incommunicative refusing food and water, then comatose. "Keep her comfortable," we were advised.

There are no mistakes you can make.

How utterly profound! Death was approachable. It was real work for the living and for the dying. There were tasks that could best be accomplished without focusing on the outcome: pain medication administered on schedule, ice chips for dry lips (a Lamaze trick, as well), a sponge bath to keep her comfortable, combing her hair away from those Scott features to freshen her brow. The mystery of Death was dispelled. There was work to do. Our hands gravitated toward the task at hand, diverting the reality that Mary was dying.

The most stunning revelation of the dying passage is the emotional act of letting go. What I did not anticipate and could not fully comprehend until it was over is this: *we all had to arrive there together.*

Mary needed our energy to accomplish the

"labor" of dying. The words, "I wish she didn't have to suffer any longer," followed by, "Yes, Yes!" opened a door that she could not open alone, and allowed her to move through the "valley of the shadow of death" into the afterlife. It was time for her to let go just as it was time for loving hands to release her.

Death as passage. This was the resolution of Mary's passage.

Victoria's passage offered a stunning confirmation of right place and right time. I knew little of her journey out—just as I had known little of her heritage here—but the mystery of her passage held its own perfection.

After the initial tidal wave of disbelief, I was able to decipher the symmetry in her wake.

"I am out of here," her spirit had said, "time to move on!" It was a breathtaking exit, the timing flawless. Her spirit had leaped over the inevitable wheelchair looming in her path with its incumbent dependency, and had soared into the hereafter. *You go girl! Yes!*

The shock I had experienced entering her abruptly empty living space was a gift as well,

Resolutions

allowing me to calm down, and to put into practice the tools I had gathered with my sisters-in-law four months earlier. I could not attend my mother's passage, but I could know its symmetry. Her "Evening Star" was the utter peace she left behind, and the dazzling Leo sun that bathed the days of details as my brothers, our sister-in-law and I gathered together the remnants of her life.

Details: there had been the physicality of cremation, then the sorting of personal effects deciding what would go to whom, what would be given away, and what could be stored and dealt with later. What to do with her clothes? What to do with the furniture and paintings? What to do with the little blue Volkswagen? Her apartment had to be made ready for inspection—carpets vacuumed the floors and bathroom scrubbed, the refrigerator cleaned out, cupboards and closets emptied.

Details, decisions, and more decisions! One step, then another, and another. Throughout it all we were, indeed, living "the best of times and the worst of times." But there was symmetry therein.

All is in Divine order. This was the resolution of Victoria's passage.

Seven months later it was Robert's time, and by then I was seasoned. I knew the terrain and I could focus on every milestone.

Flying to Maine with my soup pot and rolling pin, I knew that this would more than likely be my last shot at being a daughter. This became my *cause celebre*, my *tour de force* as I cleaned his apartment, filled his freezer with baked goods, and talked with him every morning about how we might spend the day. Every moment had to count and it did. *Thank you, Mary. Thank you, Victoria.*

All was in divine order as our focus became the microcosm of father and daughter. The time we had lost—nineteen years in real time—did not matter. The whys and wherefores and what-ifs did not matter. Moments in time freed us to create fatherhood and daughterhood anew, and that we did with as much merriment and panache as two people could muster. We were golden, my father and I. *Yes!*

Resolutions

Beer and submarines? Scrapple? The doctor says they are not really a good idea …

There are no mistakes you can make … Beer and submarines it was for supper! Scrapple with scrambled eggs for breakfast. *Yes!*

Might catch your death of cold if we go outside?

There are no mistakes you can make... We bundled up in hooded coats and scarves, loaded his oxygen tank into the back seat of the little white Escort, and off we drove into the snowy New England countryside. Yes!

A road trip and a visit too taxing?

There are no mistakes you can make... On a morning when he was feeling good, we drove over to Hetty's in Sedgwick for a lovely little lunch that she prepared for us, telling stories and laughing until his waning energy said it was time to head home. *Yes!*

I fussed over him at will, cooked his favorite foods and mine, keeping an eye on him from the passthrough window as I puttered around his kitchen.

Might I never see you again, my father?

Barbara Victoria

There are no mistakes you can make... Let us make letter writing our new "conversation!" Here is your first letter, with a folder for you to collect my thoughts and "conversations" as they come winging to Maine from Kentucky. *Yes!*

Dying? We are living, thank you. All the way!

Death as resolution was the legacy of Robert's passage. Our closure as father and daughter was complete. I did it all with him and for him in eight snowy days and nights on the coast of Maine to carry me through the weeks that followed. Within the heart of winter we had orchestrated a piece of Paradise that remains one of the perfections of my life. I am proud to this day knowing that I did something that thoroughly, something that I would not change in any way if I could.

After the year of Mary's and Victoria's and Robert's transitions, I do not fear death itself. I maintain a healthy respect for the labor of dying, just as I have a healthy respect for the labor of childbirth. I hope to engage in my own

Resolutions

transition with the same resolution that I brought to childbirth.

To do this rightly, thoroughly, depends on living well, with all the focus and grace and courage and timing that I witnessed in my loved ones who passed in one watershed year.

May I leave this earth awake and aware and in possession of every faculty I need along the way!

May I live all the way to the end! Because of Mary and Victoria and Robert, I have every reason to know that I can.

We all can.

We are all One.

Bless.

All is in divine order.

Barbara Victoria

Resolutions

Acknowledgements

Without Mary and Victoria and Robert,
there would be no story to tell.
Without Hospice there would be no insight to tell it.
Bless.

To Rogena Walden, Louise Eaton,
Pat Stuart and Ann Voll,
thank you for eagle eyes and great heart
in reading the manuscript and
providing invaluable guidance;
and Jan Woods Krier at PRODESIGN
who designed a stunning cover.
Bless.

To Annette Chaudet, my editor and
publisher at Pronghorn Press, thank you
for insight, expertise, and belief
that these stories of resolution warrant sharing.
To Dr. Doug Morton, Palliative Care Physician, and
Linda Housel, Social Worker for
Spirit Mountain Hospice, for your work and heart,
and to Bill Hoagland, writing instructor
at Northwest College for your skill and perspective.
Bless.

To Jim without whom there would be no story.
To William who believes in the story.
Bless.

Printed in the United States
38398LVS00008B/24

9 781932 636178